501 FASCINATING FACTS

PUSTAK MAHAL®
Delhi•Bangalore•Mumbai•Patna•Hyderabad•London

Publishers
Pustak Mahal®, Delhi

J-3/16 , Daryaganj, New Delhi-110002
☎ 23276539, 23272783, 23272784 • *Fax:* 011-23260518
E-mail: info@pustakmahal.com • *Website:* www.pustakmahal.com

London Office
51, Severn Crescents, Slough, Berkshire, SL 38 UU, England
E-mail: pustakmahaluk@pustakmahal.com

Sales Centre
10-B, Netaji Subhash Marg, Daryaganj, New Delhi-110002
☎ 23268292, 23268293, 23279900 • *Fax:* 011-23280567
E-mail: rapidexdelhi@indiatimes.com

Branch Offices
Bangalore: ☎ 22234025
E-mail: pmblr@sancharnet.in • pustak@sancharnet.in
Mumbai: ☎ 22010941
E-mail: rapidex@bom5.vsnl.net.in
Patna: ☎ 3294193 • *Telefax:* 0612-2302719
E-mail: rapidexptn@rediffmail.com
Hyderabad: *Telefax:* 040-24737290
E-mail: pustakmahalhyd@yahoo.co.in

© **Pustak Mahal, Delhi**

ISBN 978-81-223-0334-6

Edition : 2007

Printed at : Param Offsetters, Okhla, New Delhi-110020

Publisher's Note

'Truth is stranger than fiction' is an oft-repeated cliche, but sometimes even a cliche can turn out to be true. As has happened in the case of this compilation of '501 Fascinating Facts', published by Pustak Mahal.

At Pustak Mahal, the emphasis has always been on bringing out off-beat books of the kind that the Indian publishing industry has generally ignored, without sacrificing on quality — books that while enriching your knowledge, also provide wholesome gratification.

'501 Fascinating Facts' is another landmark in the same endeavour. Here, you will come across such facts that will astound you, amuse you, leave you shaking your head in utter disbelief, or rolling off your chair with laughter. Here, there are facts from practically every horizon of life from Science, to History, to Literature, presented in the most delectable manner.

Go through it. Don't be surprised if you find surprises in every single page!

—Publisher

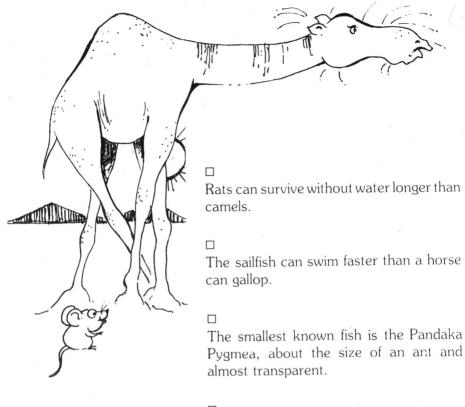

☐

Rats can survive without water longer than camels.

☐

The sailfish can swim faster than a horse can gallop.

☐

The smallest known fish is the Pandaka Pygmea, about the size of an ant and almost transparent.

☐

Men travelling through dense tropical forests often collect fireflies in jars and use them as lanterns, while women in Cuba and other tropical countries pin live fireflies on their gowns or hang them around their necks on chains as decorations.

☐

The most widely cultivated fruit in the world is the apple. The second is the pear.

☐

In the 1920s and 1930s, Charlie Chaplin was probably the most celebrated man in the world. On a visit to his native London, the motion picture comedian received 73,000 letters in just two days.

☐
There is a butterfly found in Brazil that has the smell and colour of chocolate.

☐
Neutron Bomb is a nuclear weapon, which kills people by radiation, even inside armoured vehicles, but leaves behind buildings, etc., intact.

☐
Plasma is a gas free of whole molecules and atoms and containing only ions and electrons.

☐
We blink our eyes once every six seconds i.e. in the course of a lifetime we blink about 250 million times.

☐
A dwarf, eighteen inches high, served as a captain of cavalry in the British Army. He was Jeffery Hudson and lived from 1619 to 1692.

☐
Girls tend to sleep more soundly than boys.

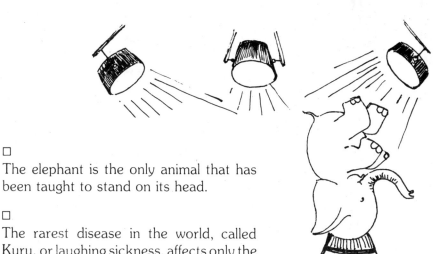

□
The elephant is the only animal that has been taught to stand on its head.

□
The rarest disease in the world, called Kuru, or laughing sickness, affects only the cannibals of New Guinea and is believed to be caused by eating human brains.

□
If a rope were made out of strands of long hair, it would be strong enough to lift an automobile.

□
Sucker fish (Remora) is nature's hitch-hiker. The upper fin of this fish is modified to form a complicated suction pad on the top of the head. The sucker fish attaches itself by means of its sucker to any passing turtle or shark, or any large fish, merely to get a free ride and in the hope of sharing a meal at the end of the journey.

□
The hottest place in the world is Dallol, Ethiopia, which has hardly any seasonal relief from high temperature.
Mean daily maximum temperature— 100°F (37.8°C)
Mean daily minimum temperature between 75°F and 89°F (24.4°C and 31.7°C)

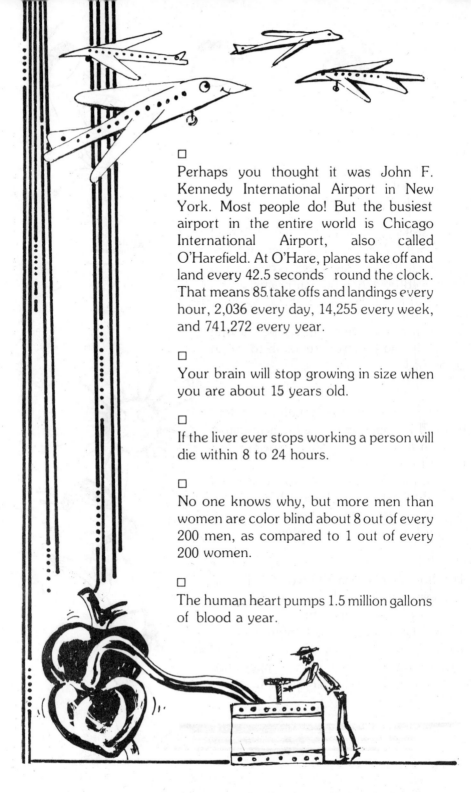

□

Perhaps you thought it was John F. Kennedy International Airport in New York. Most people do! But the busiest airport in the entire world is Chicago International Airport, also called O'Harefield. At O'Hare, planes take off and land every 42.5 seconds round the clock. That means 85 take offs and landings every hour, 2,036 every day, 14,255 every week, and 741,272 every year.

□

Your brain will stop growing in size when you are about 15 years old.

□

If the liver ever stops working a person will die within 8 to 24 hours.

□

No one knows why, but more men than women are color blind about 8 out of every 200 men, as compared to 1 out of every 200 women.

□

The human heart pumps 1.5 million gallons of blood a year.

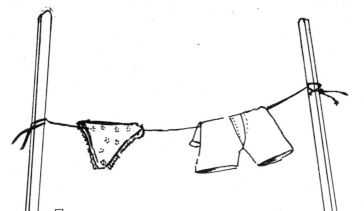

☐

In the state of Minnesota it is against the law to hang male and female underwear on the same washing line.

☐

During an 8 hour sleep, most people have from three to five dreams, each lasting from 10 to 30 minutes... and they are in colour!

☐

The shortest human being was a Dutch midget called 'Princess Pauline', who at the age of 12 was only 23.2" tall-or only 3 to 5 inches taller than a newborn baby.

☐

One psychological study has revealed that women talk about men three times as often as men talk about women.

☐

The left side of your brain controls the right side of your body and vice versa.

☐

An average person drinks about 16,000 gallons of water during his lifetime.

A sound wave travels through the air at more than 300 metres per second, or 1,100 kilometres per hour. Some jet-propelled aeroplanes far exceed the velocity of sound.

In water, sound travels roughly five times as fast as in the air. The velocity of a sound wave in water is about 1,500 metres per second, or 5,400 kilometres per hour. So far no man-made apparatus, with the exception of rockets, has attained this velocity.

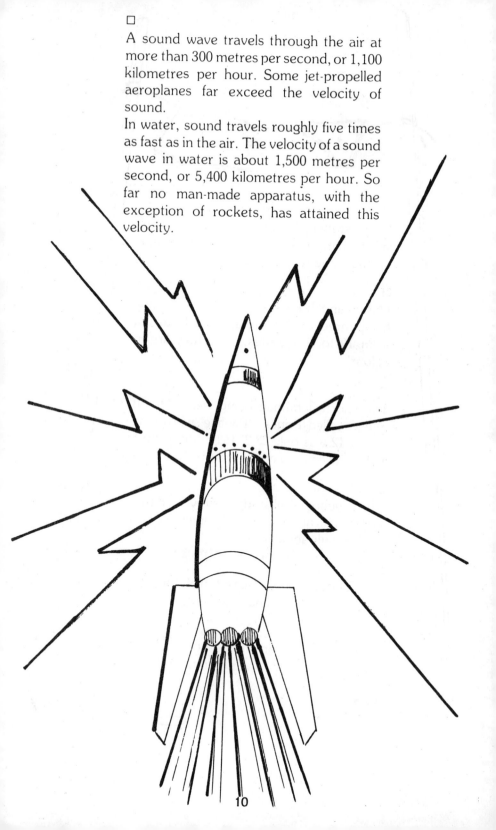

☐
A full moon is nine times brighter than a half moon.

☐
It takes about 48 hours for your body to completely digest the food from one meal.

☐
Stuttering is 4 to 6 times more common in boys than in girls.

☐
The world's most popular hobby is stamp collecting.

☐
The nerve system in the human brain has a greater number of possible connections than there would be in a unilateral telephone exchange that provided one line to every person living on earth.

☐

A snail can travel over a razor-blade without cutting itself.

☐

96 percent of babies arrive at times different from those predicted by the medical profession.

☐

Our height varies not only with years of our life, but in the course of every day. It is greatest when we get up in the morning and after the night's rest. Between morning and evening, it generally shrinks about three quarters of an inch, sometimes even more. If we have done much walking during the day, our height may shrink as much as two or three-quarter of an inch. This is due to compression of the cartilage in our spine.

☐

The average light bulb can last for about 750 to 1,000 hours.

☐

One tonne of uranium produces the same amount of energy as 30,000 tonnes of coal.

☐

The great Barrier Reef of Australia is actually the world's longest string of coral islands—more than 1250 miles long!

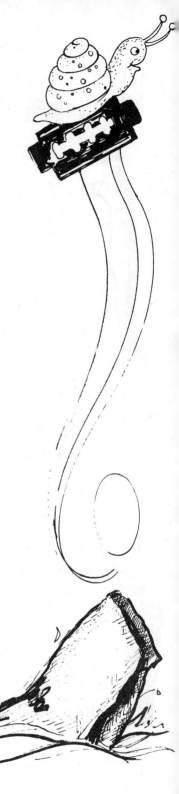

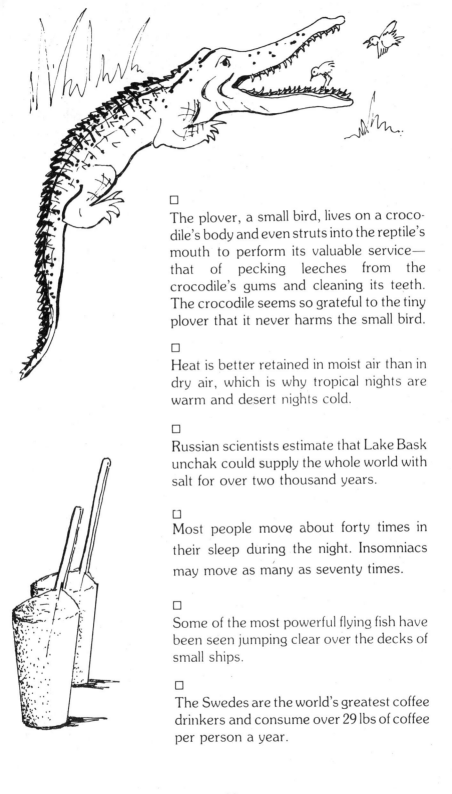

☐

The plover, a small bird, lives on a crocodile's body and even struts into the reptile's mouth to perform its valuable service—that of pecking leeches from the crocodile's gums and cleaning its teeth. The crocodile seems so grateful to the tiny plover that it never harms the small bird.

☐

Heat is better retained in moist air than in dry air, which is why tropical nights are warm and desert nights cold.

☐

Russian scientists estimate that Lake Baskunchak could supply the whole world with salt for over two thousand years.

☐

Most people move about forty times in their sleep during the night. Insomniacs may move as many as seventy times.

☐

Some of the most powerful flying fish have been seen jumping clear over the decks of small ships.

☐

The Swedes are the world's greatest coffee drinkers and consume over 29 lbs of coffee per person a year.

□

Smart bombs are highly accurate guided bombs whose accuracy was demonstrated both in the Vietnam and Middle East wars. A single bomb can destroy a difficult target.

□

A diamond is a piece of pure carbon, just as is soot in the chimney but in crystal form. It is 80 times as hard as the next hardest substance which is corundum.

□

The largest recorded single hailstone fell at Coffeyville, Kansas, U.S.A. on 3rd September 1970, and weighed 1.67 lb (758 g.) It measured 7½ in. in diameter and 17½ in. in circumference when photographed in the hands of the two boys who found it. It could have been as big as 8 in. in diameter when first picked up.

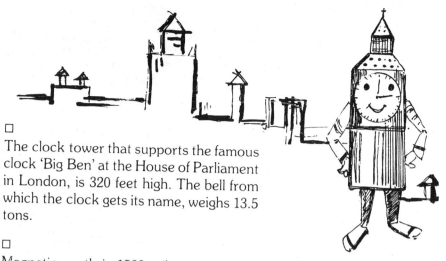

□

The clock tower that supports the famous clock 'Big Ben' at the House of Parliament in London, is 320 feet high. The bell from which the clock gets its name, weighs 13.5 tons.

□

Magnetic north is 1500 miles west of the North pole.

□

The North pole is 2,799 metres lower than the South pole.

□

If all the oceans on earth dried up the rock salt remaining would be enough to build a wall a mile thick and 18 miles high all around the equator.

□

The largest magnet in the world is the earth itself, because the hot nickel and iron at its core pull everything towards it.

□

The earth is currently inhabited by 1.4 million species of animals and 500,000 species of plants.

□

Do you know that cattlefish has three hearts, two of which are placed at the base of gills and third is the central heart.

□

There are 206 bones in the human body.

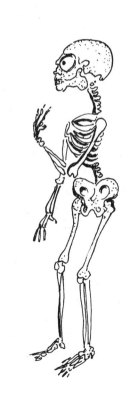

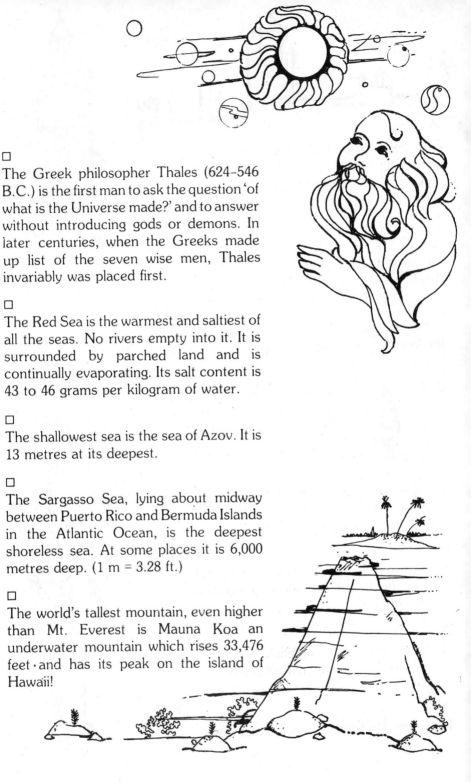

The Greek philosopher Thales (624–546 B.C.) is the first man to ask the question 'of what is the Universe made?' and to answer without introducing gods or demons. In later centuries, when the Greeks made up list of the seven wise men, Thales invariably was placed first.

The Red Sea is the warmest and saltiest of all the seas. No rivers empty into it. It is surrounded by parched land and is continually evaporating. Its salt content is 43 to 46 grams per kilogram of water.

The shallowest sea is the sea of Azov. It is 13 metres at its deepest.

The Sargasso Sea, lying about midway between Puerto Rico and Bermuda Islands in the Atlantic Ocean, is the deepest shoreless sea. At some places it is 6,000 metres deep. (1 m = 3.28 ft.)

The world's tallest mountain, even higher than Mt. Everest is Mauna Koa an underwater mountain which rises 33,476 feet · and has its peak on the island of Hawaii!

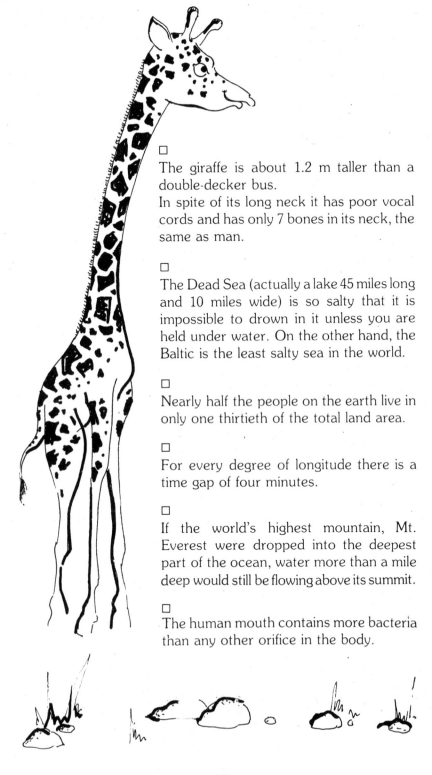

□

The giraffe is about 1.2 m taller than a double-decker bus.
In spite of its long neck it has poor vocal cords and has only 7 bones in its neck, the same as man.

□

The Dead Sea (actually a lake 45 miles long and 10 miles wide) is so salty that it is impossible to drown in it unless you are held under water. On the other hand, the Baltic is the least salty sea in the world.

□

Nearly half the people on the earth live in only one thirtieth of the total land area.

□

For every degree of longitude there is a time gap of four minutes.

□

If the world's highest mountain, Mt. Everest were dropped into the deepest part of the ocean, water more than a mile deep would still be flowing above its summit.

□

The human mouth contains more bacteria than any other orifice in the body.

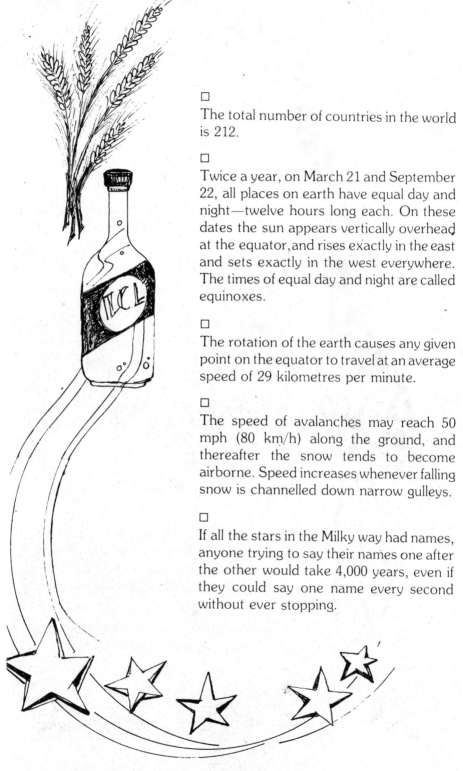

□

The total number of countries in the world is 212.

□

Twice a year, on March 21 and September 22, all places on earth have equal day and night—twelve hours long each. On these dates the sun appears vertically overhead at the equator, and rises exactly in the east and sets exactly in the west everywhere. The times of equal day and night are called equinoxes.

□

The rotation of the earth causes any given point on the equator to travel at an average speed of 29 kilometres per minute.

□

The speed of avalanches may reach 50 mph (80 km/h) along the ground, and thereafter the snow tends to become airborne. Speed increases whenever falling snow is channelled down narrow gulleys.

□

If all the stars in the Milky way had names, anyone trying to say their names one after the other would take 4,000 years, even if they could say one name every second without ever stopping.

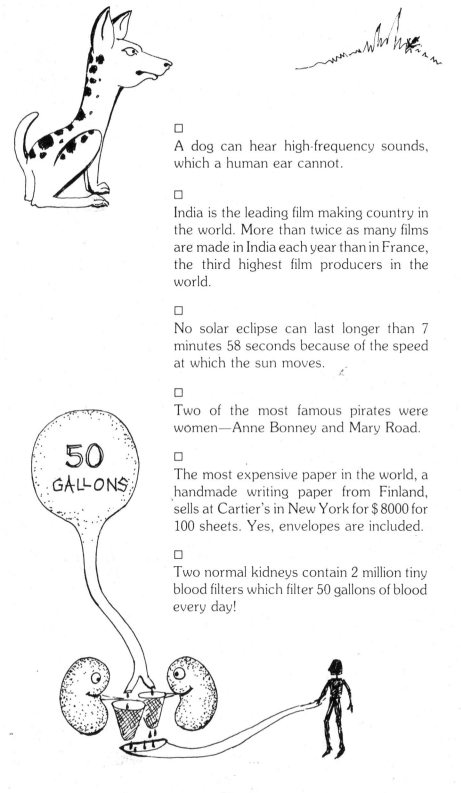

□

A dog can hear high-frequency sounds, which a human ear cannot.

□

India is the leading film making country in the world. More than twice as many films are made in India each year than in France, the third highest film producers in the world.

□

No solar eclipse can last longer than 7 minutes 58 seconds because of the speed at which the sun moves.

□

Two of the most famous pirates were women—Anne Bonney and Mary Road.

□

The most expensive paper in the world, a handmade writing paper from Finland, sells at Cartier's in New York for $ 8000 for 100 sheets. Yes, envelopes are included.

□

Two normal kidneys contain 2 million tiny blood filters which filter 50 gallons of blood every day!

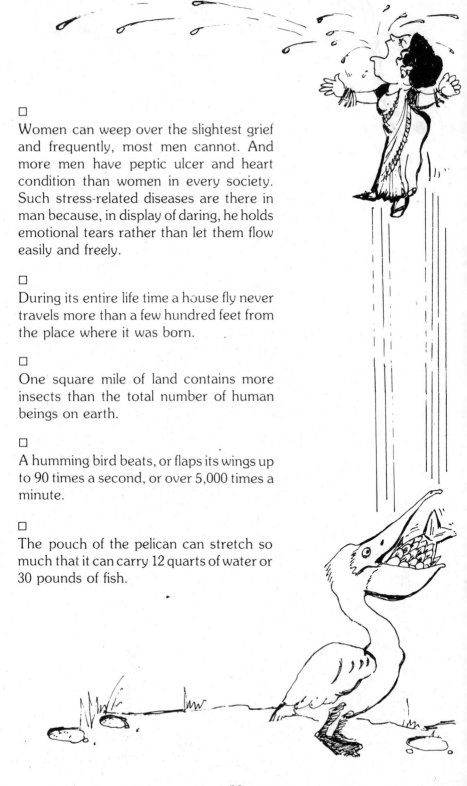

☐
Women can weep over the slightest grief and frequently, most men cannot. And more men have peptic ulcer and heart condition than women in every society. Such stress-related diseases are there in man because, in display of daring, he holds emotional tears rather than let them flow easily and freely.

☐
During its entire life time a house fly never travels more than a few hundred feet from the place where it was born.

☐
One square mile of land contains more insects than the total number of human beings on earth.

☐
A humming bird beats, or flaps its wings up to 90 times a second, or over 5,000 times a minute.

☐
The pouch of the pelican can stretch so much that it can carry 12 quarts of water or 30 pounds of fish.

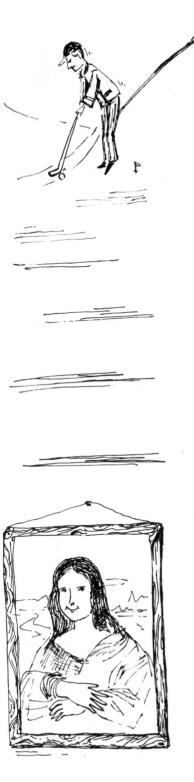

☐

There are more than 10,000 golf courses in the U.S.

☐

The altitude limit for birds is roughly the same as the summit of Mount Everest: 8,848 m above sea level.

☐

Hens can distinguish between all the colours of the rainbow.

☐

The ostrich's legs are so powerful that one kick can kill a man.

☐

Count the number of cricket chirps in 14 seconds. Add 40. The answer gives the exact temperature in degrees Fahrenheit.

☐

A scientist who weighed people immediately before and after death concluded that the human soul weighs 21 g.

☐

The Mona Lisa, now hanging in the Louvre Museum in Paris, is valued today at $ 100,000,000!

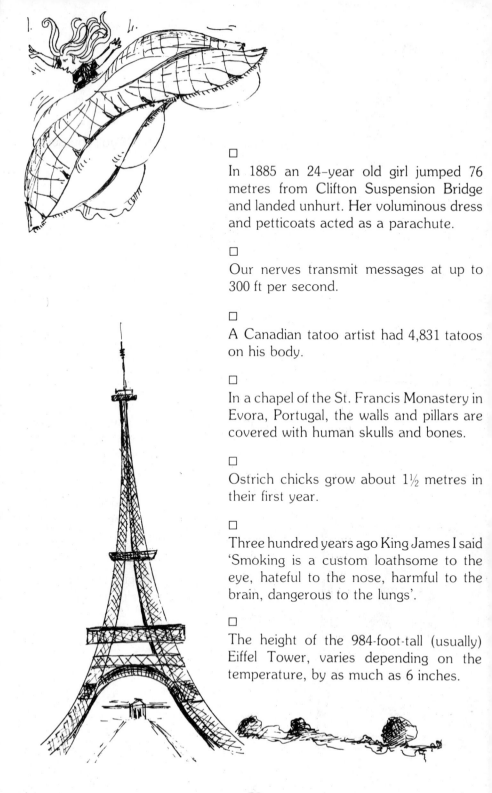

□

In 1885 an 24–year old girl jumped 76 metres from Clifton Suspension Bridge and landed unhurt. Her voluminous dress and petticoats acted as a parachute.

□

Our nerves transmit messages at up to 300 ft per second.

□

A Canadian tatoo artist had 4,831 tatoos on his body.

□

In a chapel of the St. Francis Monastery in Evora, Portugal, the walls and pillars are covered with human skulls and bones.

□

Ostrich chicks grow about 1½ metres in their first year.

□

Three hundred years ago King James I said 'Smoking is a custom loathsome to the eye, hateful to the nose, harmful to the brain, dangerous to the lungs'.

□

The height of the 984-foot-tall (usually) Eiffel Tower, varies depending on the temperature, by as much as 6 inches.

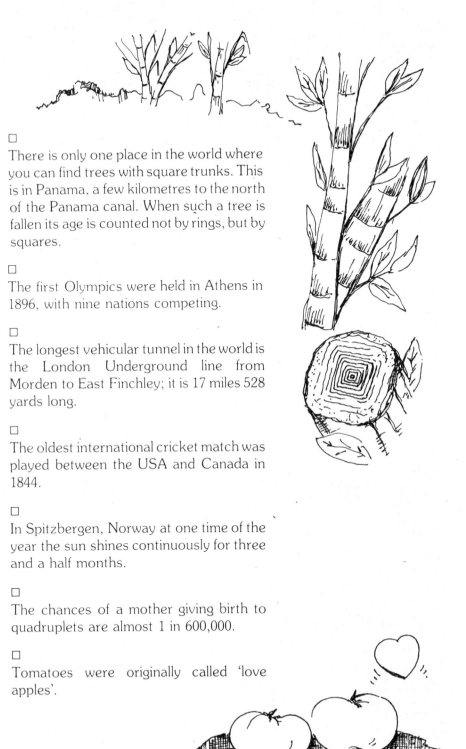

☐

There is only one place in the world where you can find trees with square trunks. This is in Panama, a few kilometres to the north of the Panama canal. When such a tree is fallen its age is counted not by rings, but by squares.

☐

The first Olympics were held in Athens in 1896, with nine nations competing.

☐

The longest vehicular tunnel in the world is the London Underground line from Morden to East Finchley; it is 17 miles 528 yards long.

☐

The oldest international cricket match was played between the USA and Canada in 1844.

☐

In Spitzbergen, Norway at one time of the year the sun shines continuously for three and a half months.

☐

The chances of a mother giving birth to quadruplets are almost 1 in 600,000.

☐

Tomatoes were originally called 'love apples'.

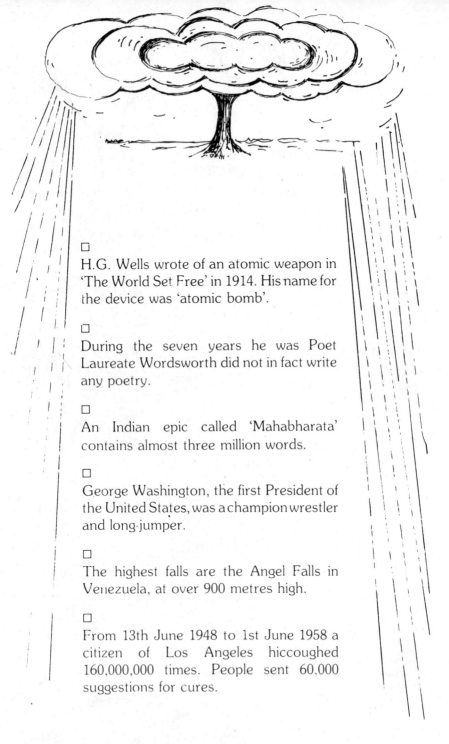

☐
H.G. Wells wrote of an atomic weapon in 'The World Set Free' in 1914. His name for the device was 'atomic bomb'.

☐
During the seven years he was Poet Laureate Wordsworth did not in fact write any poetry.

☐
An Indian epic called 'Mahabharata' contains almost three million words.

☐
George Washington, the first President of the United States, was a champion wrestler and long-jumper.

☐
The highest falls are the Angel Falls in Venezuela, at over 900 metres high.

☐
From 13th June 1948 to 1st June 1958 a citizen of Los Angeles hiccoughed 160,000,000 times. People sent 60,000 suggestions for cures.

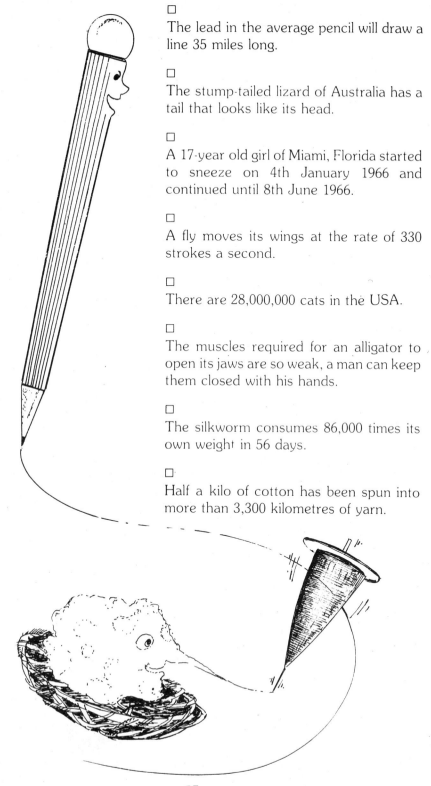

☐

The lead in the average pencil will draw a line 35 miles long.

☐

The stump-tailed lizard of Australia has a tail that looks like its head.

☐

A 17-year old girl of Miami, Florida started to sneeze on 4th January 1966 and continued until 8th June 1966.

☐

A fly moves its wings at the rate of 330 strokes a second.

☐

There are 28,000,000 cats in the USA.

☐

The muscles required for an alligator to open its jaws are so weak, a man can keep them closed with his hands.

☐

The silkworm consumes 86,000 times its own weight in 56 days.

☐

Half a kilo of cotton has been spun into more than 3,300 kilometres of yarn.

☐

Rainbows only occur when the sun is at an angle of less than 40° above the horizon.

☐

The most efficient form of light production so far discovered is the glow-worm.

☐

Four babies are born every second.

☐

It is estimated that there are 200 million left-handed people in the world.

☐

No two human outer ears (pinnae)—even your own— are exactly alike. There are some key identification points on the outer ear that do not change throughout one's life. Earology, as the system is called, was developed to supplement identification by fingerprints.

☐
Bungalows are named after the Hindi word 'bangla' which means 'belonging to Bengal'.

☐
The muscle of the human jaw exert a force of over 219 kg.

☐
The nail on our middle finger grows fastest. The nail on the thumb grows slowest.

☐
The most common disease in the world is tooth-decay.

☐
Damascus is the oldest inhabited capital city in the world.

☐
An ounce of gold can be beaten into a sheet covering 9.3 square metres, or drawn into 80.5 km (50 miles) of wire.

☐
Draftsmen have to make 27,000 drawings for the manufacture of a new car.

☐
The giant bamboos of south-east Asia can grow almost 1 metre in 24 hours.

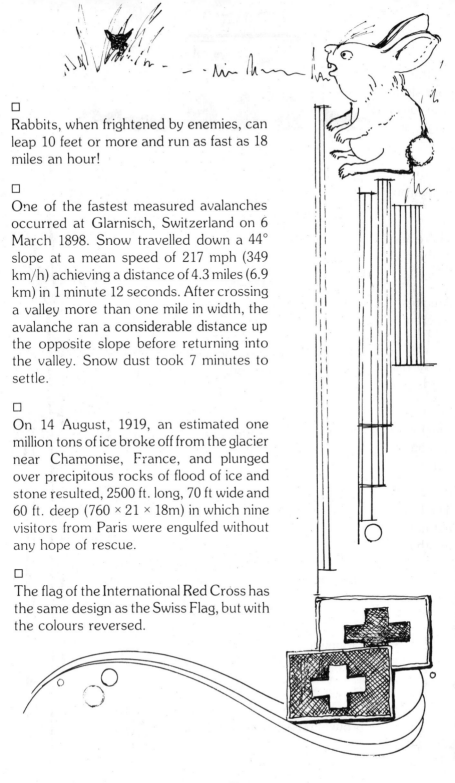

☐
Rabbits, when frightened by enemies, can leap 10 feet or more and run as fast as 18 miles an hour!

☐
One of the fastest measured avalanches occurred at Glarnisch, Switzerland on 6 March 1898. Snow travelled down a 44° slope at a mean speed of 217 mph (349 km/h) achieving a distance of 4.3 miles (6.9 km) in 1 minute 12 seconds. After crossing a valley more than one mile in width, the avalanche ran a considerable distance up the opposite slope before returning into the valley. Snow dust took 7 minutes to settle.

☐
On 14 August, 1919, an estimated one million tons of ice broke off from the glacier near Chamonise, France, and plunged over precipitous rocks of flood of ice and stone resulted, 2500 ft. long, 70 ft wide and 60 ft. deep (760 × 21 × 18m) in which nine visitors from Paris were engulfed without any hope of rescue.

☐
The flag of the International Red Cross has the same design as the Swiss Flag, but with the colours reversed.

□

Of the 22 bones connected by joints in your skull, only one can move—the one in your lower jaw, which permits you to talk, laugh, and chew food!

□

There is no cholesterol contained in Kangaroo meat.

□

There are 2,000 varieties of bats, and most of them eat insects.

□

Amongst the Arabs there are nearly 1,000 different words for a camel.

□

Every day a common shrew will eat two thirds of its own body weight.

□

Only 2,000 tigers roam wild in India today as compared to 40,000 at the turn of the century.

□

The largest of all rhinoceroses, the almost extinct white rhinoceros weighs 3½ tons and has a horn over 5 feet long!

☐

The floating island of Lake Alm in Upper Austria moves constantly from shore to shore.

☐

The record for the most weddings is held by King Mogul of Siam (the 'King' in the The King and I) who had 9000 weddings and 9000 wives.

☐

Julius Caesar gave news to his victory with the words "Veni, Vidi, Vici"—I came, I saw, I conquered.

☐

The Colossus of Rhodes which was one of the grandest of the Seven Wonders of the Ancient World, was ignominiously carried off by the Arab invaders and the bronze that had covered it was sold for scrap.

☐

The worst tornado ever recorded hurtled over Texas at a speed only slightly slower than the official World Water Speed Record, 464.45 km/h.

☐

One fifth of the oxygen we inhale is used up by the cells in the brain.

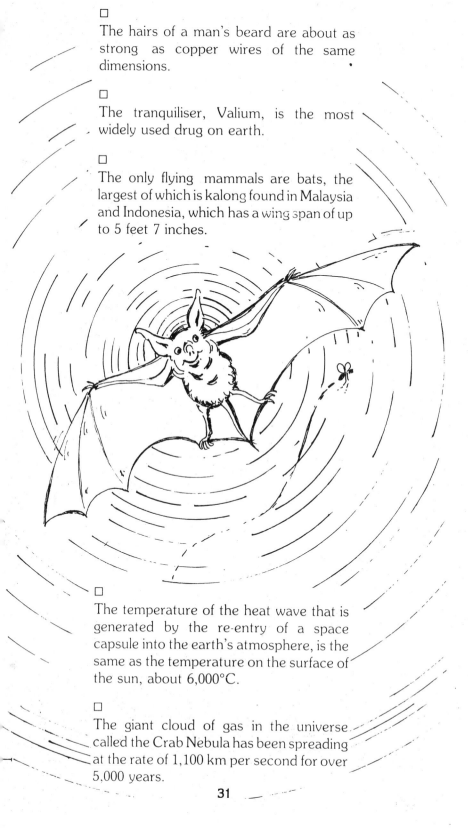

□

The hairs of a man's beard are about as strong as copper wires of the same dimensions.

□

The tranquiliser, Valium, is the most widely used drug on earth.

□

The only flying mammals are bats, the largest of which is kalong found in Malaysia and Indonesia, which has a wing span of up to 5 feet 7 inches.

□

The temperature of the heat wave that is generated by the re-entry of a space capsule into the earth's atmosphere, is the same as the temperature on the surface of the sun, about 6,000°C.

□

The giant cloud of gas in the universe called the Crab Nebula has been spreading at the rate of 1,100 km per second for over 5,000 years.

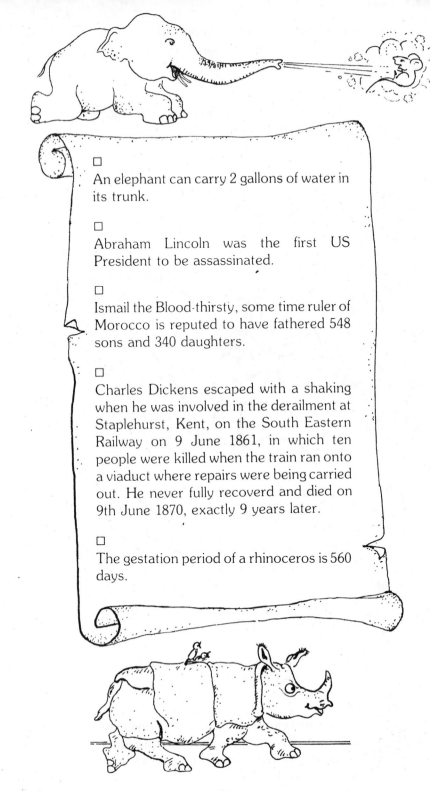

☐

An elephant can carry 2 gallons of water in its trunk.

☐

Abraham Lincoln was the first US President to be assassinated.

☐

Ismail the Blood-thirsty, some time ruler of Morocco is reputed to have fathered 548 sons and 340 daughters.

☐

Charles Dickens escaped with a shaking when he was involved in the derailment at Staplehurst, Kent, on the South Eastern Railway on 9 June 1861, in which ten people were killed when the train ran onto a viaduct where repairs were being carried out. He never fully recoverd and died on 9th June 1870, exactly 9 years later.

☐

The gestation period of a rhinoceros is 560 days.

☐

You need 120 drops of water to fill a teaspoon.

☐

In the lower depths of the oceans the water pressure is so great that a bottle dropped from the surface would be broken before it reached the bottom.

☐

It is impossible to sneeze and keep your eyes open at the same time.

☐

One of the candidates who failed at his first attempt to pass the entrance examinations for the Federal Polytechnic of Zurich was a young man named Albert Einstein.

☐

The Soviet Union is a good place for bachelors looking for prospective wives, because for every 100 women there are only 85 men to go round.

☐

The size of a newly born kangaroo is 2.5 cm.

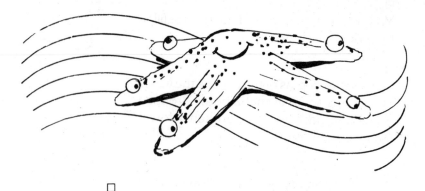

☐

The starfish has an eye on the end of each arm.

☐

The English word with the most meanings is the simple 3-letter word 'set'. It has 51 meanings as a noun, 126 meanings as a verb, and 10 meanings as a participle adjective.

☐

Experiments with ants have shown that they are capable of lifting stones fifty times their own weight and pulling loads three hundred times their own weight.

☐

Eighty percent of the animals on earth are insects.

☐

The United States Library of Congress contains 73 million volumes, housed on 350 miles of shelving.

☐
Saudi Arabia covers an area of 830,000 square miles, yet there is not a single river in the whole country.

☐
A citizen of Calcutta, India, grew the fingernails on his left hand to a length of 76 inches.

☐
A hippopotamus can run faster than a man.

☐
The humming bird can fly backwards, sideways, forwards and hover motionless for upto an hour.

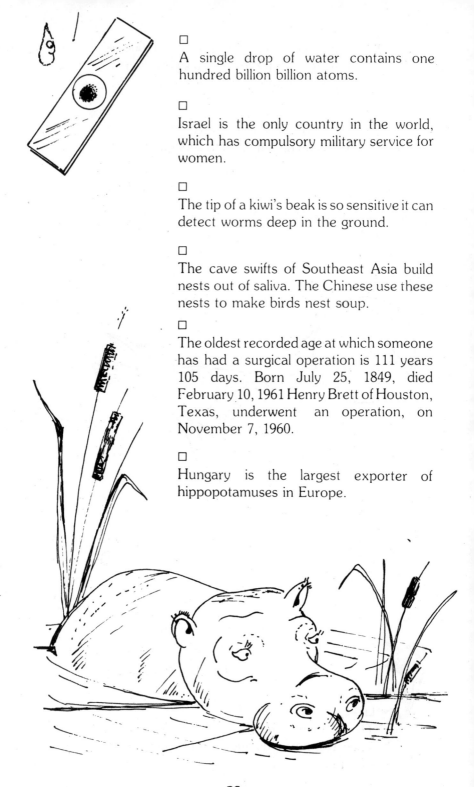

□

A single drop of water contains one hundred billion billion atoms.

□

Israel is the only country in the world, which has compulsory military service for women.

□

The tip of a kiwi's beak is so sensitive it can detect worms deep in the ground.

□

The cave swifts of Southeast Asia build nests out of saliva. The Chinese use these nests to make birds nest soup.

□

The oldest recorded age at which someone has had a surgical operation is 111 years 105 days. Born July 25, 1849, died February 10, 1961 Henry Brett of Houston, Texas, underwent an operation, on November 7, 1960.

□

Hungary is the largest exporter of hippopotamuses in Europe.

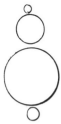

Animals sometimes can foretell natural calamities—storms, volcanic eruptions, earthquakes—sufficiently well ahead of time. Jelly-fish, for example, can sense a storm 10 to 15 hours before it actually occurs, and will leave the shore and go into deep sea.

Some Japanese households keep fish which start dashing out about the aquarium a few hours before an earthquake. Deep-sea fish on the other hand are known to rise to the surface of the water when there is an approaching calamity.

□

The frog's tongue grows from the front of its mouth which makes it easier for it to catch insects.

☐

A fish's heart has two chambers.

☐

An anagram of 'funeral' is 'real fun'.

☐

Leonardo da Vinci could write with one hand and draw with the other at the same time.

☐

The giant squid, whose length can exceed 15 metres, has the largest eyes of any living animal; they measure 38 cms across.

☐

A 14-year old French girl had extraordinary electrical powers. With a gentle touch she could knock over heavy pieces of furniture and people in physical contact with her received an electric shock.

☐

The nearest star to the earth, save the sun, is Alpha Centauri, 4.4 light years away (A light year is the distance light travels in a year at the rate of 186,000 miles per second—some six trillion miles.) The sun is only 8 light minutes away.

☐
A zebra's stripes are as individual as human fingerprints. No two zebras are striped alike.

☐
There are eight cities called Rome in the USA.

☐
The Badshahi Mosque in Lahore, Pakistan, is the largest mosque in the world, and can accommodate 100,000 in the courtyard, where services are held. It was built in 1671:

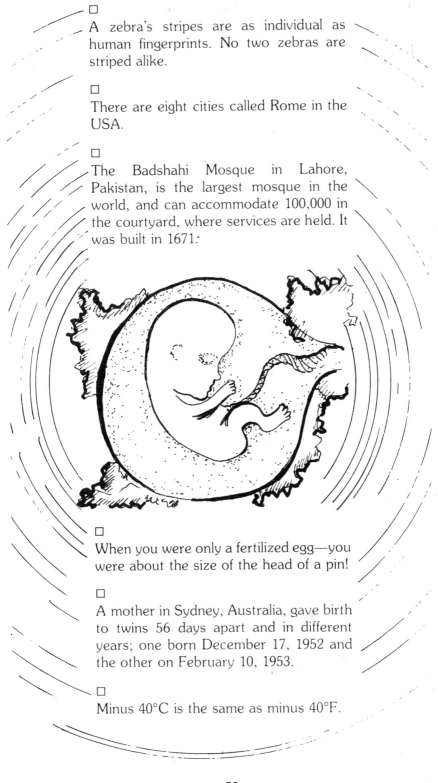

☐
When you were only a fertilized egg—you were about the size of the head of a pin!

☐
A mother in Sydney, Australia, gave birth to twins 56 days apart and in different years; one born December 17, 1952 and the other on February 10, 1953.

☐
Minus 40°C is the same as minus 40°F.

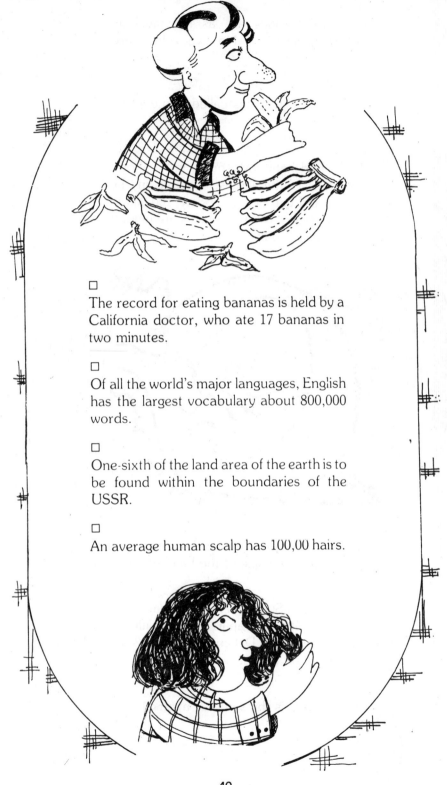

☐

The record for eating bananas is held by a California doctor, who ate 17 bananas in two minutes.

☐

Of all the world's major languages, English has the largest vocabulary about 800,000 words.

☐

One-sixth of the land area of the earth is to be found within the boundaries of the USSR.

☐

An average human scalp has 100,00 hairs.

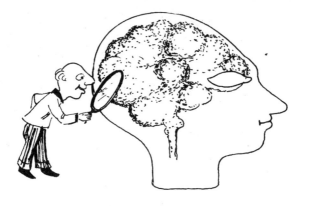

☐

Man's three-pound brain is the most complex and orderly arrangement of matter known in the universe.

☐

Our nerves transmit messages at up to 300 ft per second.

☐

We blink twenty-five times each minute.

☐

A man and woman in Mexico City were engaged for 67 years and finally married at the age of 82.

☐

The human jaw can bear more than 279 kgs. of weight.

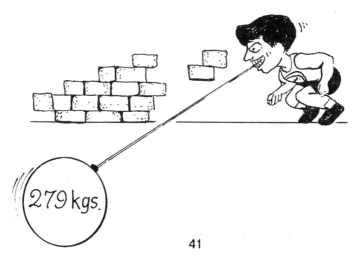

279 kgs.

☐

The earth is roughly 4600 million years old.

☐

Insects are eaten as food in many parts of the world, the favourites being grasshoppers, beetles, crickets, locusts, termites and ants.

☐

The Fennec Fox (Fennecus Zerda) from the deserts of North Africa has extremely large outer ears that conduct away excess heat.

☐

There is a street in Canada that runs for a distance of nearly 1900 kms.

☐

On average, we lose 11 oz. of weight while we are asleep at night.

☐

Ivan, the Terrible killed his favourite son in a burst of anger.

☐

The human body contains enough phosphorus to make the heads of 2000 matches, enough fat for seven bars of soap and enough iron to make one nail.

☐

The complete skin covering of the body measures about 20 square feet.

☐

The world's largest animal is the Sulphur-bottom whale which has been known to measure 150 feet in length and thirty feet in girth.

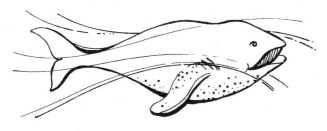

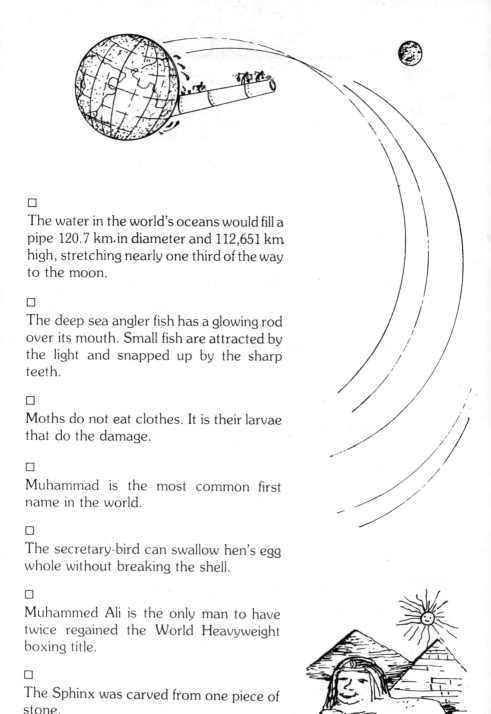

☐

The water in the world's oceans would fill a pipe 120.7 km. in diameter and 112,651 km. high, stretching nearly one third of the way to the moon.

☐

The deep sea angler fish has a glowing rod over its mouth. Small fish are attracted by the light and snapped up by the sharp teeth.

☐

Moths do not eat clothes. It is their larvae that do the damage.

☐

Muhammad is the most common first name in the world.

☐

The secretary-bird can swallow hen's egg whole without breaking the shell.

☐

Muhammed Ali is the only man to have twice regained the World Heavyweight boxing title.

☐

The Sphinx was carved from one piece of stone.

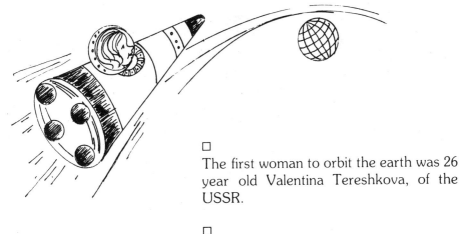

□

The first woman to orbit the earth was 26 year old Valentina Tereshkova, of the USSR.

□

One-quarter of the world's cattle live in India.

□

Nine out of ten Indian girls are married by the time they reach twenty.

□

A butterfly can look at you through 12,000 eyes.

□

In Switzerland there are more than 1,000 lakes.

□

The letter most in use in the English language is the letter 'E' and the letter 'Q' is used the least.

□

Contrary to popular belief alcohol does not warm the body but reduces body heat rapidly.

□

Chalk, which is a soft white rock, largely calcium carbonate, is formed from the shells of minute marine animals, who lived centuries ago.

☐

Every minute twelve cars are manu-
factured in the U.S.A.

☐

When a man was being hanged in
Mississippi in 1894 the noose came undone
and the prisoner fell to the ground. He was
then set free, and since his innocence was
later established he was granted, $5,000.

☐

The famous 'Siamese' twins, Chang and
Eng Bunker born in May 1811, were joined
at the chest. They married sisters, and also
died, within three hours of each other, in
January 1874.

☐

Turtles have no teeth.

☐

If goldfish are left in a dark room for a long
period they will frequently turn white.

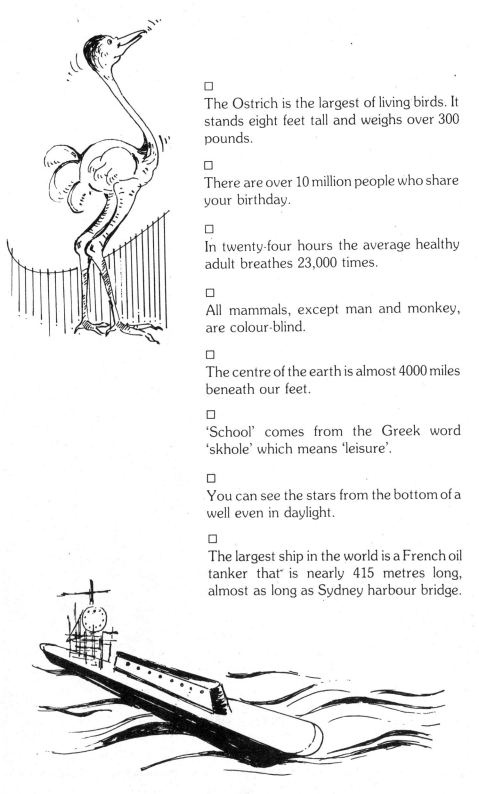

☐

The Ostrich is the largest of living birds. It stands eight feet tall and weighs over 300 pounds.

☐

There are over 10 million people who share your birthday.

☐

In twenty-four hours the average healthy adult breathes 23,000 times.

☐

All mammals, except man and monkey, are colour-blind.

☐

The centre of the earth is almost 4000 miles beneath our feet.

☐

'School' comes from the Greek word 'skhole' which means 'leisure'.

☐

You can see the stars from the bottom of a well even in daylight.

☐

The largest ship in the world is a French oil tanker that is nearly 415 metres long, almost as long as Sydney harbour bridge.

☐

Beethoven was half deaf most of his life. He was completely deaf when he composed his greatest work, the Ninth Symphony.

☐

Holland has the densest population per square mile of any nation in the world.

☐

A wingless orthopteran insect can survive in a frozen state in the Arctic for months, but dies if exposed to the warmth of a human hand.

☐

The entire contents of the first gramophone record was: 'Mary had a little lamb'.

☐

A kangaroo can hop at an estimated speed of 41 km per hour.

☐

Sir Winston Churchill's last words were: 'Oh, I am so bored, with it all'.

☐

The word 'karate' means 'empty hand'.

☐

In the Great Fire of London in 1666 only six people died.

☐

Salt was once a very precious commodity, so much so that many people were paid their wages in salt hence the word 'salary'.

☐

The lowest valued note in the world is the Hong Kong 1 cent note of which 1,200 equal £ 1.00.

☐
The sun weighs 330,000 times as much as the earth.

☐
The first atomic submarine Nautillus was launched in 1954.

☐
The Sahara is as large as Europe and larger than the combined area of the next nine largest deserts in the world.

☐
Up to 30,000 tonnes of cosmic dust are deposited on the earth each year.

☐
Flies take off with a backward jump.

☐
Fireflies are bright enough to shine through the stomach of a frog.

☐
Three 25 watt bulbs produce less light than one 75 watt bulb.

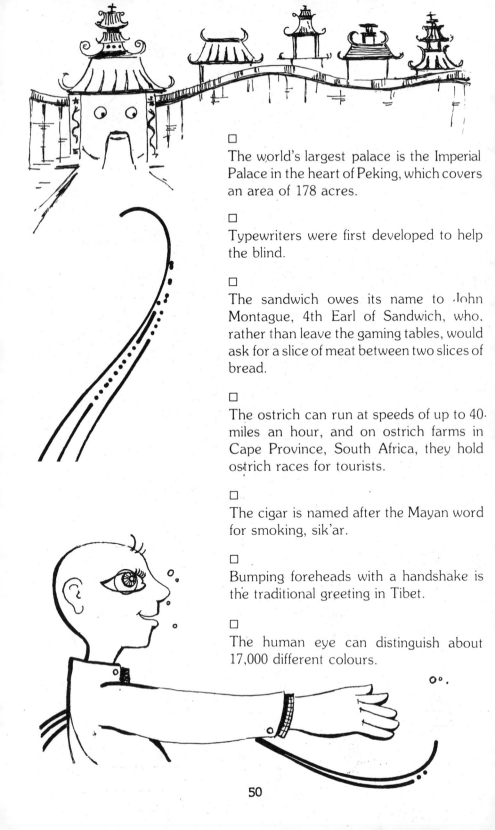

☐

The world's largest palace is the Imperial Palace in the heart of Peking, which covers an area of 178 acres.

☐

Typewriters were first developed to help the blind.

☐

The sandwich owes its name to John Montague, 4th Earl of Sandwich, who, rather than leave the gaming tables, would ask for a slice of meat between two slices of bread.

☐

The ostrich can run at speeds of up to 40 miles an hour, and on ostrich farms in Cape Province, South Africa, they hold ostrich races for tourists.

☐

The cigar is named after the Mayan word for smoking, sik'ar.

☐

Bumping foreheads with a handshake is the traditional greeting in Tibet.

☐

The human eye can distinguish about 17,000 different colours.

□

There is more sugar in a kilo of lemons than in a kilo of strawberries.

□

If you had fifteen books on a shelf and you arrange them in every possible combination, and if you made one change every minute, it would take you 2,487,996 years to do them all.

□

In the twelfth century Henry I decreed that a yard was to equal the distance from the end of his nose to the end of his thumb.

□

It was claimed that a tiger shot by Colonel Jim Corbett in 1907 had killed 436 people in India.

□

A rattle snake or viper has special cells between its nostril and its eye which are sensitive to infra-red radiant heat. They can locate people in the dark by the heat they give off.

□

The Emperor Penguin of the Antarctic can reach a depth of 870 feet and remain submerged for as long as 18 minutes.

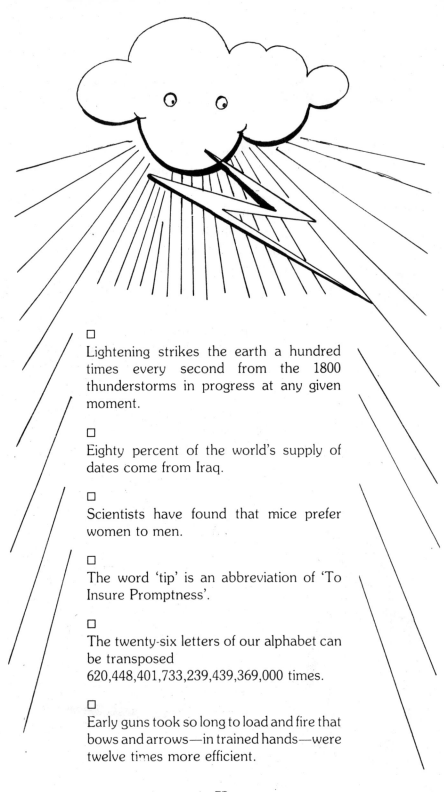

☐
Lightening strikes the earth a hundred times every second from the 1800 thunderstorms in progress at any given moment.

☐
Eighty percent of the world's supply of dates come from Iraq.

☐
Scientists have found that mice prefer women to men.

☐
The word 'tip' is an abbreviation of 'To Insure Promptness'.

☐
The twenty-six letters of our alphabet can be transposed 620,448,401,733,239,439,369,000 times.

☐
Early guns took so long to load and fire that bows and arrows—in trained hands—were twelve times more efficient.

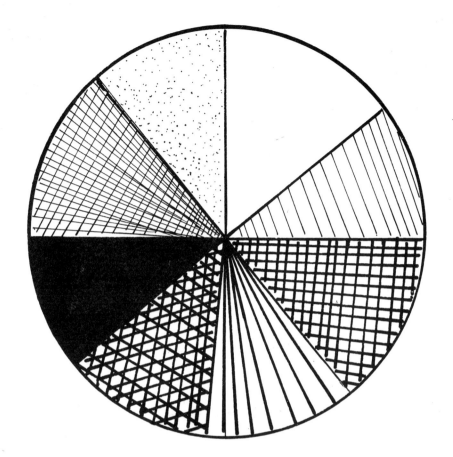

□
Primary colours—red, yellow and blue—
are so called because they cannot be
obtained by mixing any other colour, but
secondary colours can be produced by
mixing any two of these together in equal
amounts. (Red + Yellow = Orange, Red +
Blue = Violet, Yellow + Blue = Green)
Intermediate colours are obtained when
one primary and one secondary colours
are mixed together in equal amounts.
There are in all six intermediate colours.

□

When they would raid Siberia in the months of darkness, the Mongols had an ingenious method for finding their way home in the dark. They would leave at their camp the young foals of their mares. After the raid, the riders would drop the reins, and the mares instinctively carried them straight back to the foals.

□

After Spartacus's gladiatorial revolt had been suppressed in 71 B.C. no less than 6000 recaptured slaves were crucified on miles of crosses all along Rome's main highway, the Appian Way.

☐

The silkworm is not a worm. It is a caterpillar.

☐

The fourth mughal Emperor, Jahangir, who ruled from 1605 to 1627, had a harem of 300 royal wives, 5,000 more women, and 1,000 young men for alternate pleasures. Outside the palace, he stabled other kinds of pets: 12,000 elephants, 10,000 oxen, 2,000 camels, 3,000 deer, 4,000 dogs, 100 tame lions, 500 buffaloes and 10,000 carrier pigeons.

☐

Each square inch of human skin consists of 19 million cells, sixty hairs, ninety oil glands, nineteen feet of blood vessels, 625 sweat glands, and 19,000 sensory cells.

☐

The driest place on Earth is Calama, in the Atacama Desert in Chile. Not a drop of rain has been seen there.

☐

Every year more than 50,000 earthquakes take place on earth. Of these most are too slight to be noticeable to man.

☐

There are 2,500,000 rivets in the Effel Tower.

☐

People who have never married are 7½ times more likely to be hospitalized in a state or community psychiatric facility than those who are married.

☐

Peter the Great had his wife's lover executed and his head put into a jar of alcohol. She had to keep it in her bedroom.

☐

There are more than 600 muscles in our muscular system.

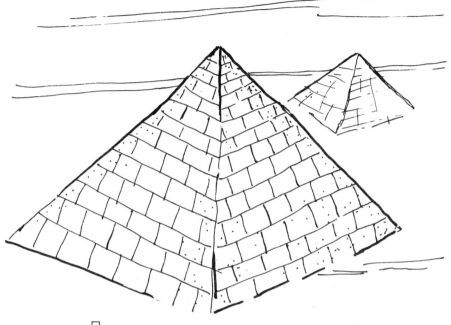

☐

Of the Seven Wonders of the Ancient World, only one, the Pyramids of Egypt, is still in existence. Others have crumbled and disappeared. The great reason of the duration of the pyramid above all other forms is, that it is most fitted to resist the force of gravitation.

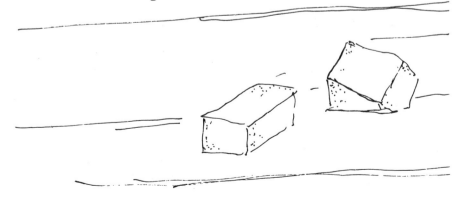

□

The royal house of Saudi Arabia may at present have as many as 5,000 princes and an equal number of princessess. King Abdul Aziz Saud, who ruled from 1932 until his death in 1953, had 300 wives.

□

Coffee is the world's second largest item of international commerce. (petroleum is first).

□

House Lizards are perfectly harmless. They neither bite nor are they aggressive. In fact they help man by eating insects like flies and mosquitoes.

□

A popular misconception seems to be that filtered cigarettes are less dangerous than unfiltered ones. According to a study the opposite would be the case: people who prefer filtered cigarettes are in danger of dying two to almost four years earlier than smokers of filterless cigaretts. Filters prevent the dilution of the smoke by oxygen so that the bloodstream builds up higher levels of carbon monoxide, in the form of carboxyhemoglobin.

□

Egyptian embalmers used to remove a dead person's brains through his nostrils.

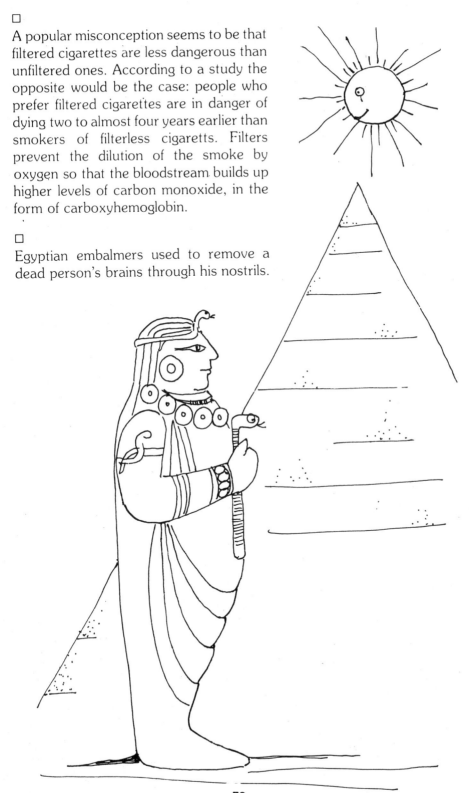

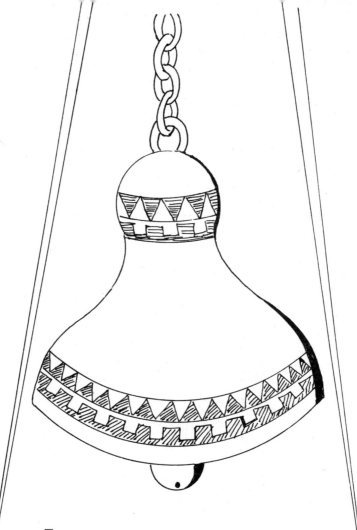

□

The heaviest bell in the world, the Tsar Kolokol Bell, was cast in 1733 in Moscow, Russia. This bell, which has been standing in the Kremlin since 1836, is over 19 feet high, 24 inches thick, and weighs 216 tons.

□

A person's hair cannot turn white overnight because of some terrible tragedy or frightening experience—or for any other reason.

☐

Tycho Brahe, the most prominent astronomer of the late sixteenth century, was extraordinarily quarrelsome and arrogant. Over a point in mathematics, he foolishly engaged in a midnight duel that cost him his nose. He was only nineteen at the time (1565). For the rest of his life (thirty-six years) he wore a false nose of metal.

☐

Assembly line methods made it possible for the U.S. Shipyards of Henry J. Kaiser during World War II to produce a ship in just four ys.

□

The luckiest number in Italy is 13.

□

The sphinx was carved from one piece of stone.

□

Every tenth egg is larger than the preceding nine.

□

When a piece of glass cracks, the cracks move at a speed of over 4,800 kms per hour.

☐

The most talkative parrot on record, an African grey parrot belonging to a London family, had a vocabulary of almost 1000 words.

☐

Most people move about forty times in their sleep during the night. Insomniacs may move as many as seventy times.

☐

The camel has no gall bladder.

☐

The famous Egyptian sphinx is in fact a statue of the goddess Armachis.

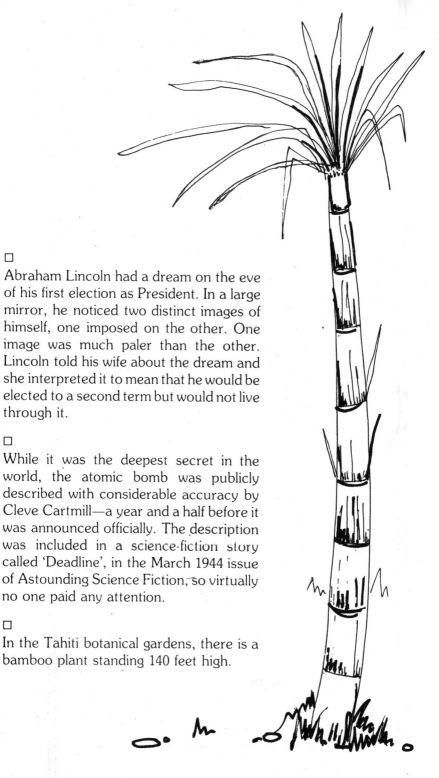

□

Abraham Lincoln had a dream on the eve of his first election as President. In a large mirror, he noticed two distinct images of himself, one imposed on the other. One image was much paler than the other. Lincoln told his wife about the dream and she interpreted it to mean that he would be elected to a second term but would not live through it.

□

While it was the deepest secret in the world, the atomic bomb was publicly described with considerable accuracy by Cleve Cartmill—a year and a half before it was announced officially. The description was included in a science-fiction story called 'Deadline', in the March 1944 issue of Astounding Science Fiction, so virtually no one paid any attention.

□

In the Tahiti botanical gardens, there is a bamboo plant standing 140 feet high.

□

Napoleon suffered from ailurophobia, the fear of cats.

□

The complete root system of the Pumpkin plant would stretch for 24 kilometres, if every root was laid end to end.

□

In 1695, two scientists obtained a diamond from a rich patron and heated it by using a lens to focus light on it. The diamond disappeared. Diamond is made of carbon, and it burns just as coal will when it is heated strongly enough.

□

Winston Churchill was born in a ladies' cloakrom in the ancestral castle of Blenheim. His mother was attending a dance there when she prematurely delivered.

☐

It was proposed in the Rhode Island legislature in the 1970s that there be enacted a $2 tax on every act of sexual intercourse.

☐

The first motion picture copyrighted in the United States showed a man in the act of sneezing. (The year was 1894).

☐

The social instinct among monkeys is so strong that if one of a group is ill, the others will forego their food etc. for him.

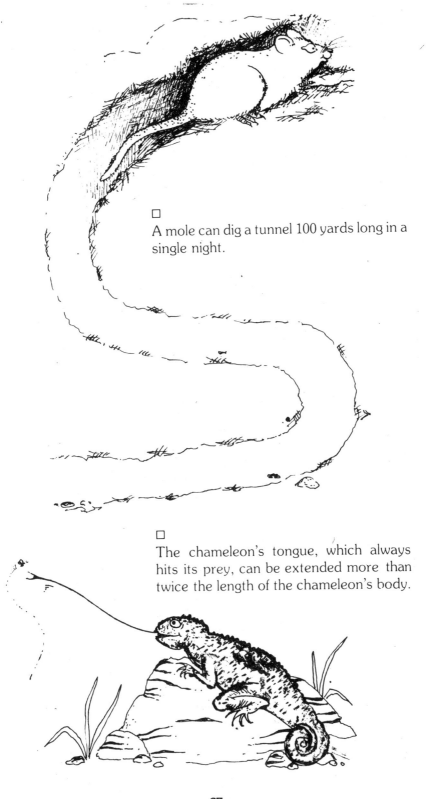

☐
A mole can dig a tunnel 100 yards long in a single night.

☐
The chameleon's tongue, which always hits its prey, can be extended more than twice the length of the chameleon's body.

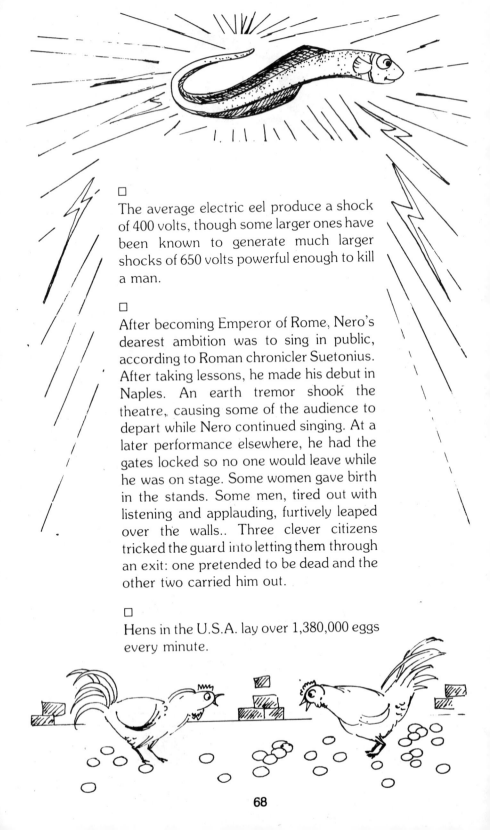

☐

The average electric eel produce a shock of 400 volts, though some larger ones have been known to generate much larger shocks of 650 volts powerful enough to kill a man.

☐

After becoming Emperor of Rome, Nero's dearest ambition was to sing in public, according to Roman chronicler Suetonius. After taking lessons, he made his debut in Naples. An earth tremor shook the theatre, causing some of the audience to depart while Nero continued singing. At a later performance elsewhere, he had the gates locked so no one would leave while he was on stage. Some women gave birth in the stands. Some men, tired out with listening and applauding, furtively leaped over the walls.. Three clever citizens tricked the guard into letting them through an exit: one pretended to be dead and the other two carried him out.

☐

Hens in the U.S.A. lay over 1,380,000 eggs every minute.

☐

The greater Dwarf Lemur of Madagascar always give birth to triplets.

☐

Blind people who have been blind from birth cannot dream sights but they dream sounds instead.

☐

Pornography is a $ 4 billion business in the U.S. annually.

☐

Eskimos use refrigerators to keep food from freezing.

☐

When the 'mad monk' Rasputin was assassinated in Petrograd (Leningrad) in 1916, his assassins first fed him cakes and wine laced with enough cyanide to kill several men. Rasputin ate and drank, and showed no ill effects. Then Prince Felix Yussupov shot him through the chest and clubbed him on the head with a lead-filled walking stick, and the conspirators threw him into the Neva River. When the body was recovered, the autopsy revealed that Rasputin had drowned.

☐

The jeep got its name from its original initials G. P. which stood for General Purpose Vehicle.

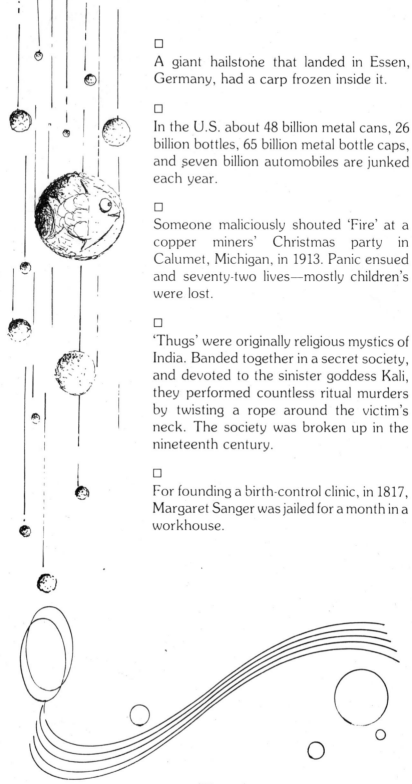

☐

A giant hailstone that landed in Essen, Germany, had a carp frozen inside it.

☐

In the U.S. about 48 billion metal cans, 26 billion bottles, 65 billion metal bottle caps, and seven billion automobiles are junked each year.

☐

Someone maliciously shouted 'Fire' at a copper miners' Christmas party in Calumet, Michigan, in 1913. Panic ensued and seventy-two lives—mostly children's were lost.

☐

'Thugs' were originally religious mystics of India. Banded together in a secret society, and devoted to the sinister goddess Kali, they performed countless ritual murders by twisting a rope around the victim's neck. The society was broken up in the nineteenth century.

☐

For founding a birth-control clinic, in 1817, Margaret Sanger was jailed for a month in a workhouse.

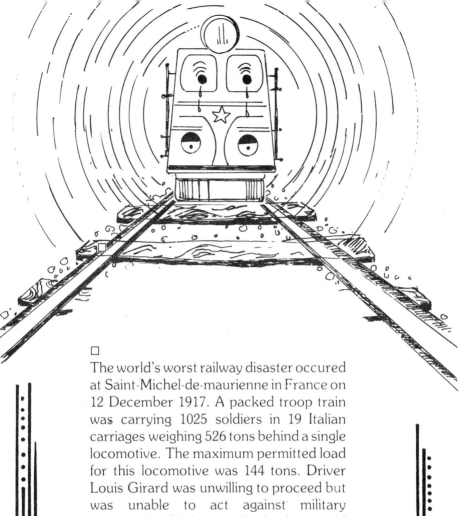

□

The world's worst railway disaster occured at Saint-Michel-de-maurienne in France on 12 December 1917. A packed troop train was carrying 1025 soldiers in 19 Italian carriages weighing 526 tons behind a single locomotive. The maximum permitted load for this locomotive was 144 tons. Driver Louis Girard was unwilling to proceed but was unable to act against military commands. Of the 543 dead who could be accounted for in the wreckage 135 could not be identified. The driver miraculously survived and was freed of all blames.

□

14622047999 divided by 10 leaves a remainder of 9 divided by 9 leaves a remainder of 8 divided by 8 leaves a remainder of 7 etc.

☐
Abraham Lincoln was convinced all his life that he, like his mother Nancy Hanks, was illegitimate, and generally smarter, shrewder and more intelligent people than others. Not until after his assassination was it proved that Lincoln had been legitimate.

☐
Chemically the substance that is closest to human blood is sea water.

☐
Luminous bacteria, that have the ability to give off light have been cooled to a temperature of –190°C and found to be alive when they were warmed up.

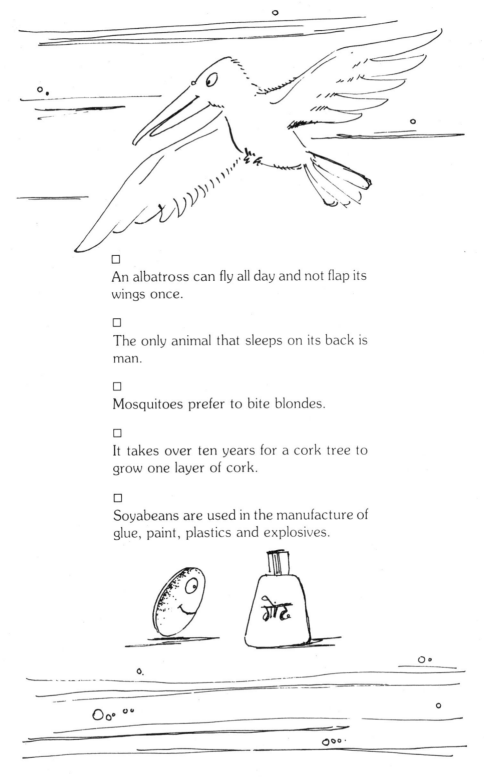

☐

An albatross can fly all day and not flap its wings once.

☐

The only animal that sleeps on its back is man.

☐

Mosquitoes prefer to bite blondes.

☐

It takes over ten years for a cork tree to grow one layer of cork.

☐

Soyabeans are used in the manufacture of glue, paint, plastics and explosives.

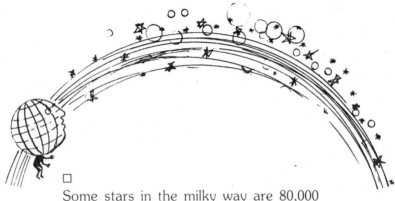

☐

Some stars in the milky way are 80,000 light years from the earth.

☐

The human body contains enough fat to make seven bars of soap.

☐

Petrol and paraffin extinguish fires in bales of cotton more efficiently than water.

☐

Grasshoppers have white blood.

☐

Christian Heinrich of Lubeck was able to talk when he was eight weeks old and he knew pieces from the Pentateuch and the Bible at the age of thirteen months.

☐

An Alsatian's sense of smell is a million times better than a man's.

□

The Great White Shark is the only creature living in the sea that has no natural enemies even killer whales avoid it.

□

The sentence, "The quick brown fox jumps over the lazy dog", contains all the letters of the alphabet.

□

At an altitude of 7,620 metres a pilot can see for a distance of 312 kilometres.

□

A female mosquito can produce 150,000,000 offspring in one year.

□

.Taiwan is the largest exporter of mushrooms in the world.

☐
Rain contains Vitamin B_{12}.

☐
The Mona Lisa was first bought by Francis I King of France, who used it to decorate his bathroom.

☐
The largest eggs are laid by sharks.

☐
There are 3,000 sweat glands to every square inch of skin in the palms of our hands.

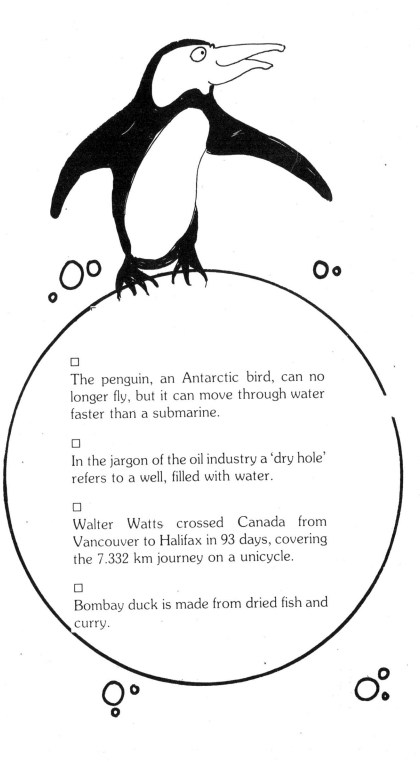

☐
The penguin, an Antarctic bird, can no longer fly, but it can move through water faster than a submarine.

☐
In the jargon of the oil industry a 'dry hole' refers to a well, filled with water.

☐
Walter Watts crossed Canada from Vancouver to Halifax in 93 days, covering the 7.332 km journey on a unicycle.

☐
Bombay duck is made from dried fish and curry.

☐

Miss Fanny Miles of Cincimario Ohio, U.S.A. had feet that were 60 cms long.

☐

Sodium burns fiercely when placed in water but it can be stored quite safely in paraffin.

☐

Windsor Castle is the largest inhabited castle in the world.

☐

The giant bamboos of south-east Asia can grow almost one metre in 24 hours.

☐

Banana oil does not come from bananas, it is a chemical distillate obtained from coal.

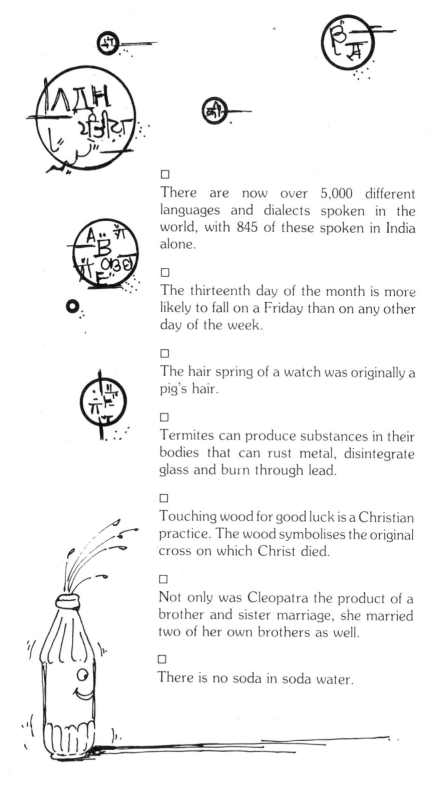

☐

There are now over 5,000 different languages and dialects spoken in the world, with 845 of these spoken in India alone.

☐

The thirteenth day of the month is more likely to fall on a Friday than on any other day of the week.

☐

The hair spring of a watch was originally a pig's hair.

☐

Termites can produce substances in their bodies that can rust metal, disintegrate glass and burn through lead.

☐

Touching wood for good luck is a Christian practice. The wood symbolises the original cross on which Christ died.

☐

Not only was Cleopatra the product of a brother and sister marriage, she married two of her own brothers as well.

☐

There is no soda in soda water.

□

Any whole number decreased by the sum of its digits will leave a remainder that can be divided by 9.

□

There are at least eighty different varieties of rice grown in India.

□

The superstitions surrounding the number 13 originate from the last supper, when 13 sat down to eat.

□

A yak has the skeleton of a bison, the hair of a goat, the tail of a horse, the head of a cow and makes a grunt like a pig.

□

What we call Indian ink actually comes from China.

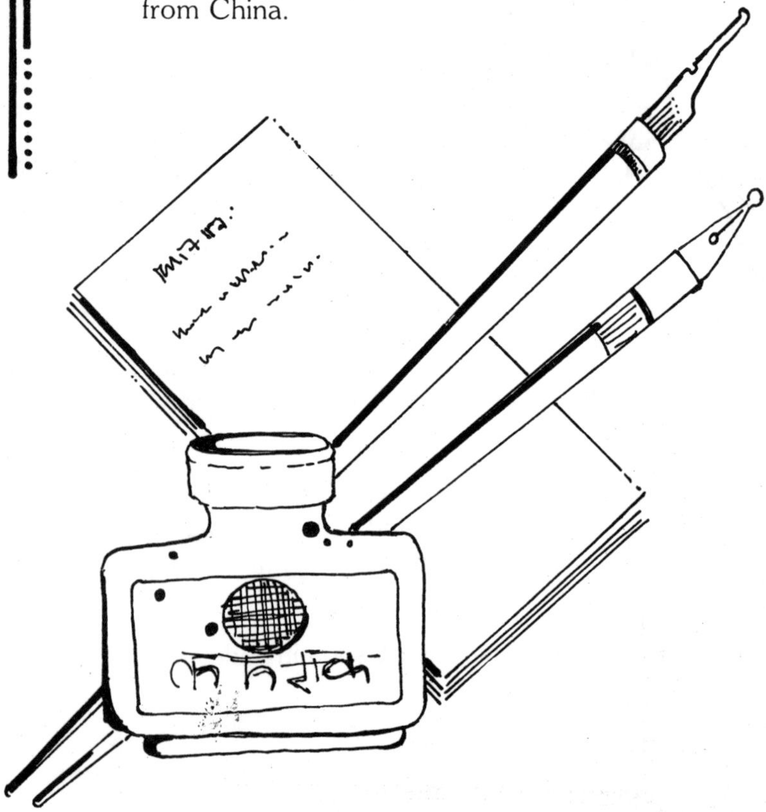

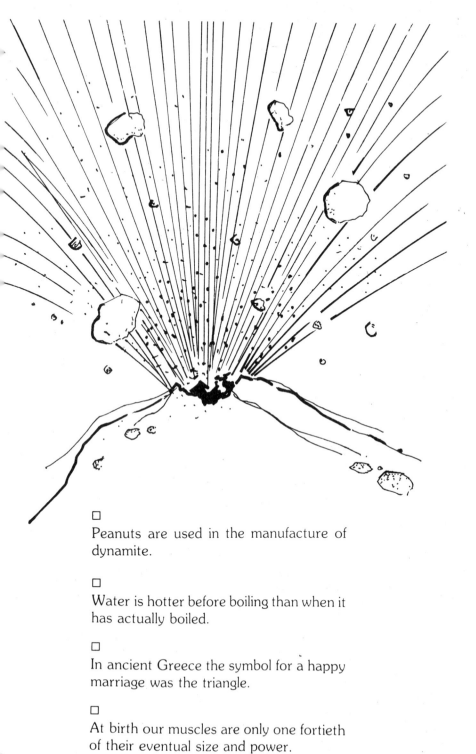

☐
Peanuts are used in the manufacture of dynamite.

☐
Water is hotter before boiling than when it has actually boiled.

☐
In ancient Greece the symbol for a happy marriage was the triangle.

☐
At birth our muscles are only one fortieth of their eventual size and power.

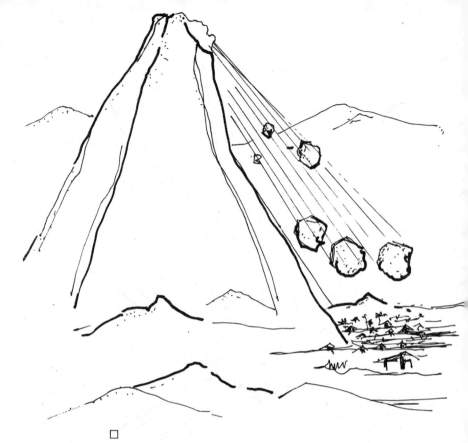

☐

On January 1962 an estimated four million tons of ice avalanched from the 22,205 ft. (6768 m) peak of Navado de Huascaran, Peru, S. America. As the avalanche continued downhill, it gathered up rocks and mud as well, travelling a total distance of 11 miles at an estimated speed of 60 m.p.h. in about 15 minutes. Seven villages, one town and about 3500 persons were wiped out in this short space of time, as well as an estimated 10,000 livestock.

☐

Birds are sometimes able to set their own broken wings.

☐

There is a waterfall near Honolulu which 'falls' upwards.

Every country in the world has its name printed on its stamps — except Great Britain — the first to issue them!

☐

The word 'Amen' is the Hebrew word for 'so be it'. It is used by Christians, Jews and Moslems as well.

☐

Both Alexander the Great and Julius. Caesar were epileptics.

☐

The sun burns 240,000,000 tonnes of hydrogen dust every minute.

The Taj Mahal, one of the world's most beautiful buildings, was scheduled to be torn down in the 1930s so that its marble facing could be removed and shipped to London for sale by auction to the landed English gentry. Wrecking machinery was moved into the garden grounds and work about to begin when word came from London not to proceed.

The backbone of a camel is perfectly straight.

Adrienne Cuyot of Belgium was engaged 652 times and married 53 times over a period of 23 years.

Haj Ahmel, who was once Bey of Algeria, had 385 wives who all came from different parts of the world so that none of them could communicate.

When Mohammed Ali was ruler of Egypt he created two infantry regiments consisting solely of one-eyed soldiers.

Otters cause no splash when they plunge into the water.

□

You have about 3,000 taste buds on your tongue!

□

The rainbow trout makes its nest from pebbles which it carries in its mouth.

□

The twenty-first wife of Hieronymus of Rome had been married twenty times before.

□

There is a city in the Sahara called Tegazza which is built entirely of salt.

□

The funeral processing of a Chinese general marched 3,700 kilometres and lasted for a whole year.

□

The nail on your middle finger grows fastest. Your thumb nail is the slowest to grow.

□

11^2	$=121$
111^2	$=12321$
1111^2	$=1234321$
11111^2	$=123454321$

□

A cat's eyes glow at night because they have a layer of cells in the inner eye that reflect light.

□

There are more than 200 different viruses that can cause colds!

□

If a drop of whisky is squirted onto its back, a scorpion will sting itself to death.

□

The income tax rate for the Gulf states of Bahrain, Kuwait and Qatar is nil.

□

Any five digit number multiplied by 11 and then multiplied by 9091 will reappear twice in the product.

□

Tests have shown that the combination of black and yellow has the strongest visual impact, black on white follows next.

□

Nearly all our weather is produced in the lower 15 km of the the atmosphere.

□

Eating mice that had been fried alive used to be regarded as a cure for smallpox in many parts of Britain.

□

Many breeds of tropical fish could survive in an aquarium filled with human blood.

□

Most people can distinguish 10,000 different smells.

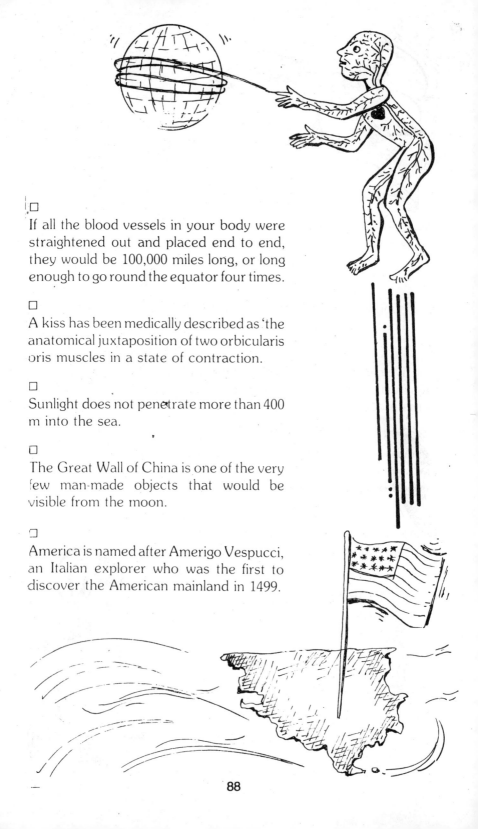

☐
If all the blood vessels in your body were straightened out and placed end to end, they would be 100,000 miles long, or long enough to go round the equator four times.

☐
A kiss has been medically described as 'the anatomical juxtaposition of two orbicularis oris muscles in a state of contraction.

☐
Sunlight does not penetrate more than 400 m into the sea.

☐
The Great Wall of China is one of the very few man-made objects that would be visible from the moon.

☐
America is named after Amerigo Vespucci, an Italian explorer who was the first to discover the American mainland in 1499.

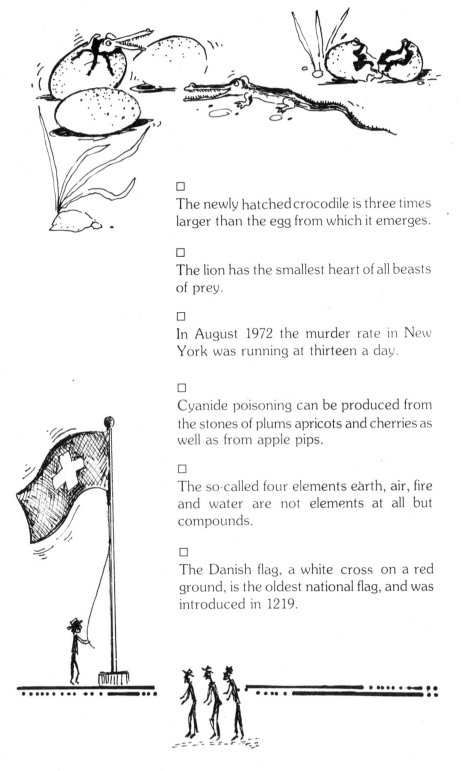

☐

The newly hatched crocodile is three times larger than the egg from which it emerges.

☐

The lion has the smallest heart of all beasts of prey.

☐

In August 1972 the murder rate in New York was running at thirteen a day.

☐

Cyanide poisoning can be produced from the stones of plums apricots and cherries as well as from apple pips.

☐

The so-called four elements earth, air, fire and water are not elements at all but compounds.

☐

The Danish flag, a white cross on a red ground, is the oldest national flag, and was introduced in 1219.

☐
An owl cannot see in total darkness.

☐
Cubes of ice insulated in glass-fibre have been baked in an oven at 190° without melting.

☐
The silk used by spiders to weave their webs is stronger than steel drawn out to form a thread of the same diameter.

☐
During the seven years that he was poet laureate William Wordsworth never wrote a line of poetry.

☐
A shark's skeleton is made of cartilage, it has no bone.

☐
Lead and tin melt at 326.6°C and 230°C respectively.

☐
The elephant is the only animal with four knees.

☐
Cattle can be identified by their noseprints just as men can be identified by their finger prints.

☐
The cheetah is the fastest animal over a short distance. Up to 600 metres it can run at 113 kph.

☐
The question mark ? developed from the early practice of putting the first and last letters of word 'questio' after a sentence. As this practice increased the 'q' was written above the 'o' until finally the 'q' degenerated into ? and the 'o' became simply (.).

☐
There is one type of ice that does not melt—dry ice. It evaporates.

☐
Elephants cannot jump.

☐
It is possible to mix oil and water. All you have to do is add a little soap.

☐
The explosive charge of the first atom bomb was packed into a tube 7.6 cm long. When it exploded however, it had the same effect as 20,000 tonnes of TNT.

☐
Fireflies are not flies and glow-worms are not worms. They are all beetles.

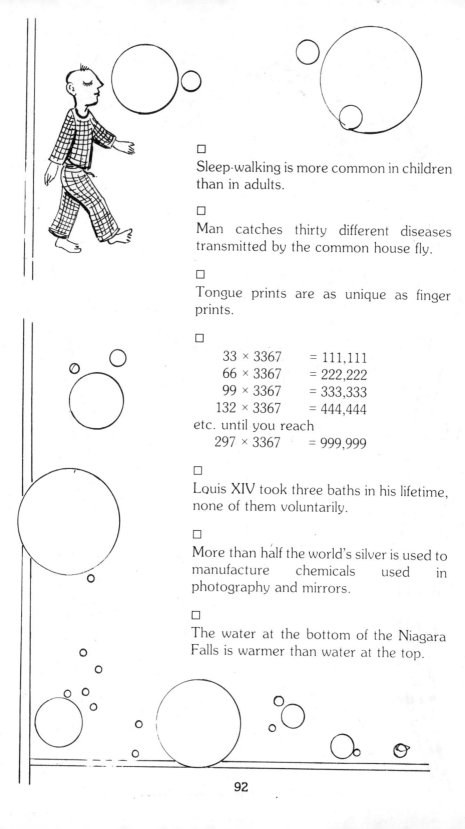

□

Sleep-walking is more common in children than in adults.

□

Man catches thirty different diseases transmitted by the common house fly.

□

Tongue prints are as unique as finger prints.

□

33 × 3367	= 111,111
66 × 3367	= 222,222
99 × 3367	= 333,333
132 × 3367	= 444,444

etc. until you reach

297 × 3367	= 999,999

□

Louis XIV took three baths in his lifetime, none of them voluntarily.

□

More than half the world's silver is used to manufacture chemicals used in photography and mirrors.

□

The water at the bottom of the Niagara Falls is warmer than water at the top.

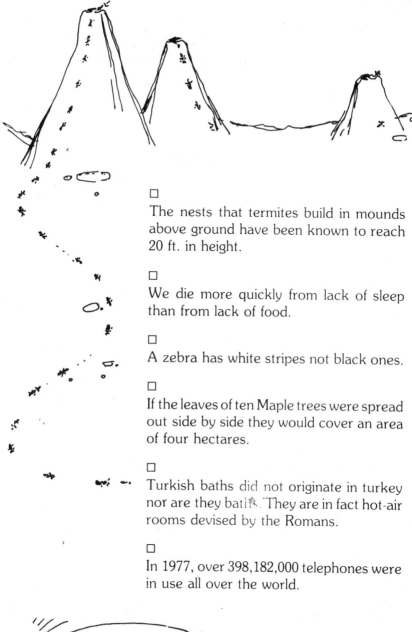

□

The nests that termites build in mounds above ground have been known to reach 20 ft. in height.

□

We die more quickly from lack of sleep than from lack of food.

□

A zebra has white stripes not black ones.

□

If the leaves of ten Maple trees were spread out side by side they would cover an area of four hectares.

□

Turkish baths did not originate in turkey nor are they baths. They are in fact hot-air rooms devised by the Romans.

□

In 1977, over 398,182,000 telephones were in use all over the world.

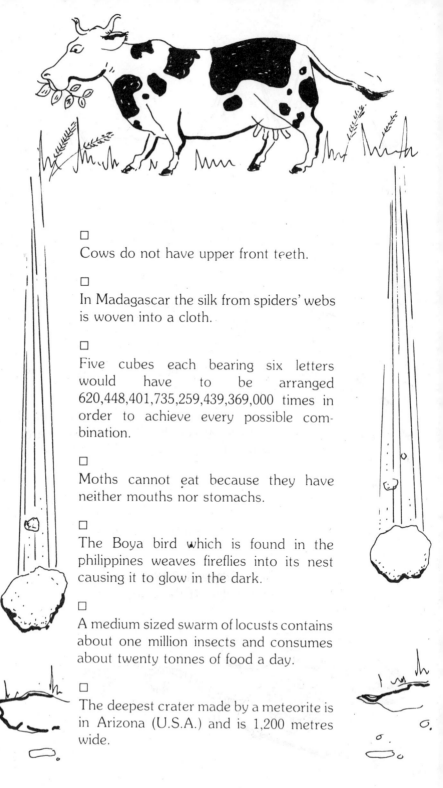

☐

Cows do not have upper front teeth.

☐

In Madagascar the silk from spiders' webs is woven into a cloth.

☐

Five cubes each bearing six letters would have to be arranged 620,448,401,735,259,439,369,000 times in order to achieve every possible combination.

☐

Moths cannot eat because they have neither mouths nor stomachs.

☐

The Boya bird which is found in the philippines weaves fireflies into its nest causing it to glow in the dark.

☐

A medium sized swarm of locusts contains about one million insects and consumes about twenty tonnes of food a day.

☐

The deepest crater made by a meteorite is in Arizona (U.S.A.) and is 1,200 metres wide.

☐

A queen bee only leaves her hive to lead out a swarm and to go on her wedding flight.

☐

A kiwi's beak is so sensitive that it can detect the presence of worms deep in the soil.

☐

Hot water pipes freeze more easily than pipes carrying cold water.

☐

Cockroaches have remained unchanged on earth for about 250,000,000 years.

☐

Ships travel faster in cold water than in warm water.

☐

The word 'love' used for scoring in tennis is a corruption of the French word 'l'oeuf which was French slang for zero because the symbol looked like an egg.

☐

The Vinegar river, in Columbia contains so much sulphuric acid and hydrochloric acid that it is so sour that no fish can live in it.

☐

The tallest people in the world are the men of the Watutsi tribe of Central Africa, who are often 2.3 metres tall.

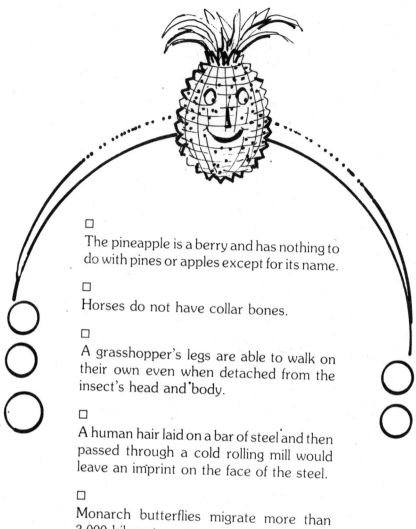

☐
The pineapple is a berry and has nothing to do with pines or apples except for its name.

☐
Horses do not have collar bones.

☐
A grasshopper's legs are able to walk on their own even when detached from the insect's head and body.

☐
A human hair laid on a bar of steel and then passed through a cold rolling mill would leave an imprint on the face of the steel.

☐
Monarch butterflies migrate more than 3,000 kilometres every year.

☐
Male mosquitoes do not bite only the females.

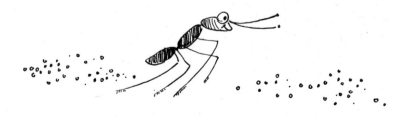

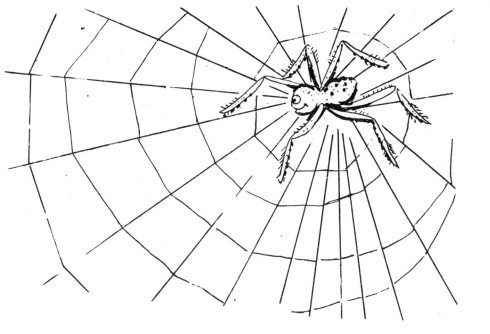

☐
There is enough nutritional value in leather to keep a human alive for a short time. So when in doubt nibble your wallet or handbag.

☐
Spiders are able to manufacture anaesthetics, glue, glue-proof oil and silk· within their bodies.

☐
As a clock unwinds it loses weight.

☐
A blind and handicapped Scotsman, William McPherson was able to read with his tongue.

☐
The Guinea-pig is not a pig and does not come from Guinea. It is a South American rodent.

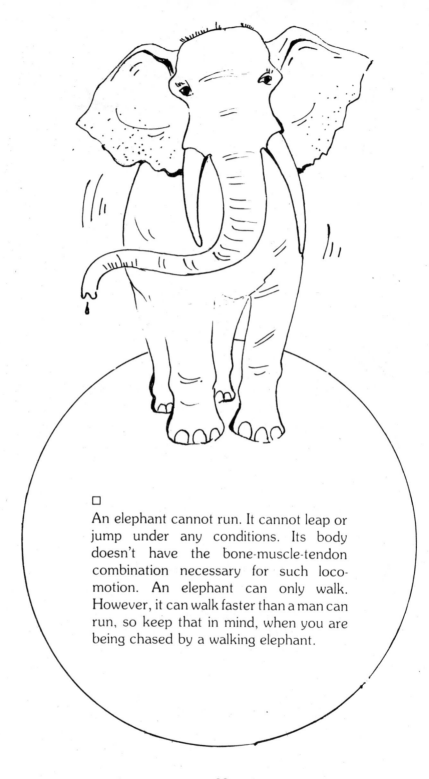

☐

An elephant cannot run. It cannot leap or jump under any conditions. Its body doesn't have the bone-muscle-tendon combination necessary for such loco-motion. An elephant can only walk. However, it can walk faster than a man can run, so keep that in mind, when you are being chased by a walking elephant.

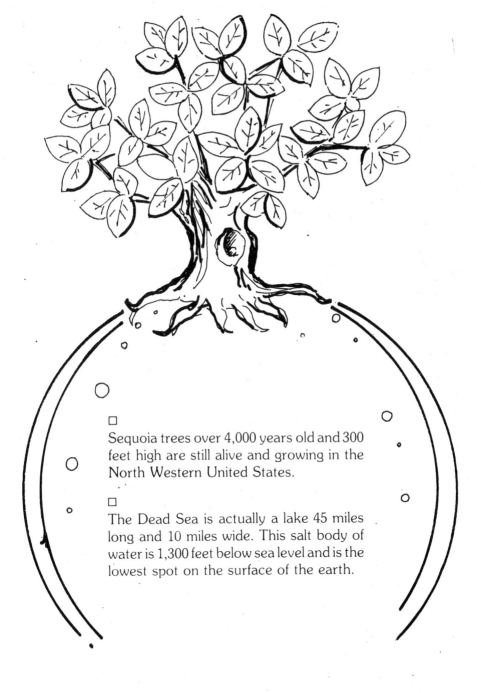

□
Sequoia trees over 4,000 years old and 300 feet high are still alive and growing in the North Western United States.

□
The Dead Sea is actually a lake 45 miles long and 10 miles wide. This salt body of water is 1,300 feet below sea level and is the lowest spot on the surface of the earth.

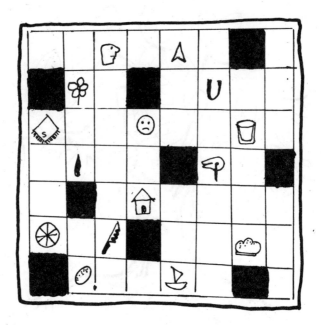

□

In 1926, a waiter in a coffee house in Budapest committed suicide. The police had to ask for help from the public in deciphering the suicide note, which was in the form of a crossword.

□

The normal worker bee has to visit nearly 1,500 flowers in order to fill its honey sac. In a good season one beehive might store as much as a kilo of honey each day, which involves about five million individual bee journeys.

□

The Mediterranean is the bluest sea. Its blue, limpid water is poor in fish food, plankton. This is why the catches are small in it.

□

26 countries in the world have no coastline at all.

☐
The human mouth produces 2-3 pints of a saliva a day.

☐
A sea urchin walks on the ends of its teeth.

☐
You can tell a fish's age by counting the rings on its scales in the same way that you can estimate the age of a tree by counting the rings in the trunk.

☐

It takes seventeen muscles to smile and forty three muscles to frown.

☐

Saudi Arabia imports sand from Scotland and camels from North Africa.

☐

The Archer Fish can catch flies by spitting at them.

☐

Water dissolves more substances than any other liquid.

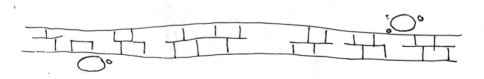

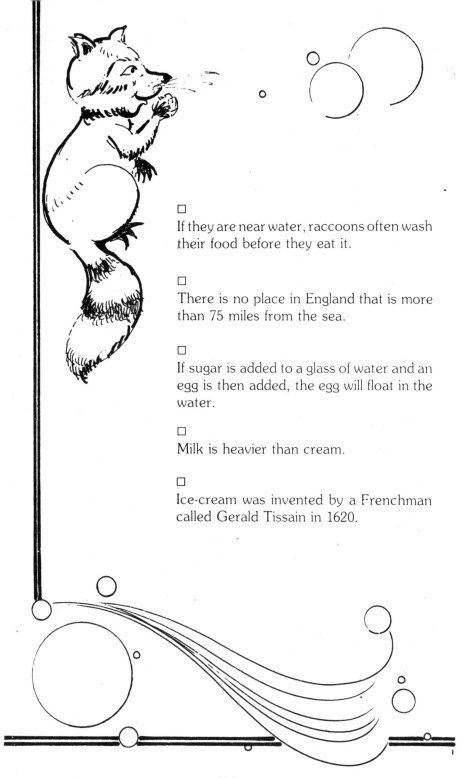

☐

If they are near water, raccoons often wash their food before they eat it.

☐

There is no place in England that is more than 75 miles from the sea.

☐

If sugar is added to a glass of water and an egg is then added, the egg will float in the water.

☐

Milk is heavier than cream.

☐

Ice-cream was invented by a Frenchman called Gerald Tissain in 1620.

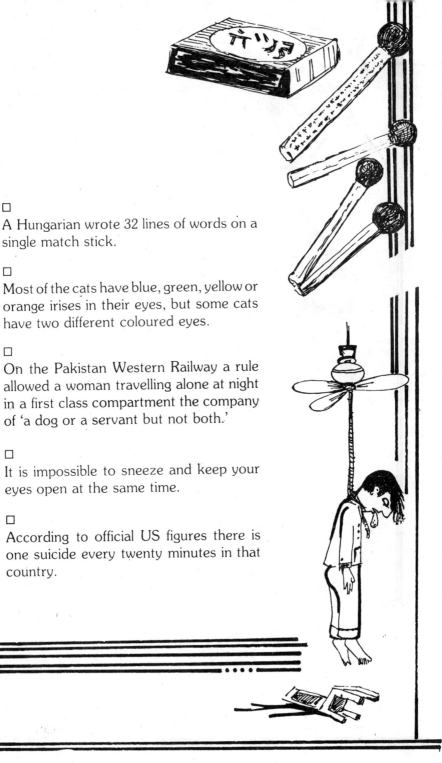

□

A Hungarian wrote 32 lines of words on a single match stick.

□

Most of the cats have blue, green, yellow or orange irises in their eyes, but some cats have two different coloured eyes.

□

On the Pakistan Western Railway a rule allowed a woman travelling alone at night in a first class compartment the company of 'a dog or a servant but not both.'

□

It is impossible to sneeze and keep your eyes open at the same time.

□

According to official US figures there is one suicide every twenty minutes in that country.

Rapidex Courses & General Knowledge

"रैपिडैक्स" इंगलिश स्पीकिंग कोर्स

price **138/-** each

The course is available with audio cassette separately in: **Hindi, Gujarati, Telugu, Tamil, Marathi, Bangla, Kannada, Nepali, Malayalam, Assamese, Oriya, Urdu, *Gurmukhi, *Arabic and Sinhelese**.

*Without Audio Cassette/CD ** Rs. 320/- (Without Audio Cassette/CD)

FREE CD with Hindi only

Rapidex Language Learning Course

A 12-Volume series teaching 6 Regional Languages through Hindi & vice versa

हिन्दी-बंगला लर्निंग कोर्स

price **96/-** each

Hindi Learning Courses through Regional Languages	Regional Language Learning Courses through Hindi
Bangla-Hindi	Hindi-Bangla
	Hindi-Gujarati
Malayalam-Hindi	Hindi-Malayalam
Tamil-Hindi	Hindi-Tamil
Kannada-Hindi	Hindi-Kannada
Telugu-Hindi	Hindi-Telugu

Rapidex Computer Course

step-by-step self learning kit

Price: **220/-** each

FREE GIFTS — Tutorial CD, Mouse Pad & Google User Guide

Children's Knowledge Bank

A tonic to your child's brain

Also available in Hindi

SAVE 20% Pay Rs. 300/- instead of Rs. 360/- for complete set of 6 books priced Rs.60/- each

Children's Science Library

Also available in Hindi

SAVE 20% Pay Rs. 350/- instead of Rs. 425/- for complete set of 17 books priced Rs.25/- each

Easiest and simplest way to make useful projects...

Rapidex DTP Course

Price: **96/-**

Price: **150/-**

71 +10 New Science Projects Self-learning Kit

Price: **120/-** each

FREE CD

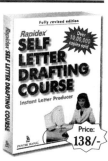

Fully revised edition

Rapidex SELF LETTER DRAFTING COURSE — Instant Letter Producer

Over 10,00,000 copies sold

Price: **138/-**

Self-Improvement

152 pp • Rs. 96/-

128 pp • Rs. 96/-

168 pp • Rs. 120/-

104 pp • Rs. 80/-

376 pp • Rs. 150/-

240 pp • Rs. 96/-

136 pp • Rs. 96/-

240 pp • Rs. 120/-

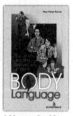
128 pp • Rs. 80/-
Also available in Hindi

144 pp • Rs. 96/-

155 pp • Rs. 80/-

292 pp • Rs. 150/-

156 pp • Rs. 80/-

312 pp • Rs. 96/-

176 pp • Rs. 120/-

192 pp • Rs. 96/-

160 pp • Rs. 96/-

140 pp • Rs. 80/-

64 pp • Rs. 60/-
Also available in Hindi

136 pp • Rs. 80/-
Also available in Hindi

168 pp • Rs. 120/-

96 pp • Rs. 80/-

80 pp • Rs. 68/-
Also available in Hindi

208 pp • Rs. 96/-

160 pp • Rs. 80/-
Also available in Hindi

192 pp • Rs. 96

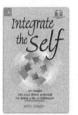
112 pp • Rs. 120
With CD

120 pp • Rs. 75/-
Earlier printed as
Teens to Twenties

176 pp • Rs. 68/-

140 pp • Rs. 60/-

Self-Improvement/Career & Management

174 pp • Rs. 88/-

140 pp • Rs. 80/-

192 pp • Rs. 96/-

184 pp • Rs. 96/-

138 pp • Rs. 80/-

180 pp • Rs. 80/-

168 pp • Rs. 96/-

112 pp • Rs. 95/-

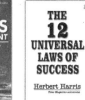
192 pp • Rs. 195/-

136 pp • Rs. 80/-

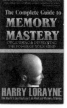
312 pp • Rs. 160/-

128 pp • Rs. 60/-

176 pp • Rs. 96/-

304 pp • Rs. 120/-

128 pp • Rs. 80/-

140 pp • Rs. 96/-

176 pp • Rs. 80/-

176 pp • Rs. 68/-

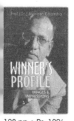
128 pp • Rs. 120/-

120 pp • Rs. 80/-

128 pp • Rs. 96/-

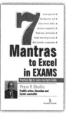
160 pp • Rs. 80/-
Also available in Hindi

144 pp • Rs. 80/-

172 pp • Rs. 125/-

136 pp • Rs. 96/-

184pp • Rs. 120/-

128 pp • Rs. 96/-

208 pp • Rs. 225/-

100 pp • Rs. 150/-

128 pp • Rs. 80/-

132 pp • Rs. 120/-

120 pp • Rs. 80/-

392 pp • Rs. 60/-

144 pp • Rs. 96/-

200 pp • Rs. 88/-

200 pp • Rs. 96/-

106 pp • Rs. 80/-

248 pp • Rs. 150/-

336 pp • Rs. 175/-

192 pp • Rs. 150/-

128 pp • Rs. 96/-

160 pp • Rs. 95/-

240 pp • Rs. 195/-

176 pp • Rs. 150/-

96 pp • Rs. 96/-

472 pp • Rs. 450/-

280 pp • Rs. 175/-

240 pp • Rs. 195/-

136 pp • Rs. 80/-

192 pp • Rs. 120/-

184 pp • Rs. 88/-

200 pp • Rs. 80/-

256 pp • Rs. 120/-

152 pp • Rs. 96/-

160/- pp • Rs. 88/-

208 pp • Rs. 96/-

280 pp • Rs. 195/-

136 pp • Rs. 96/-

288 pp • Rs. 96/-

& many more...

Children's Knowledge Bank

Fully Revised &
Updated
Redesigned in Full Colour

890 Articles

800 Illustrations

800 Pages

SAVE Rs. 101
Pay Rs. 599/- instead of
Rs. 700/- for complete
set of 4 volumes price
Rs. 175/- each

Also available in Hindi

232 pp • Rs. 135/-

128 pp • Rs. 88/-

84 pp • Rs. 50/-

120 pp • Rs. 80/-

136 pp • Rs. 80/-

136 pp • Rs. 80/-

112 pp • Rs. 120/-
oloured Ed. + FREE Tutorial CD

New

168 pp • Rs. 125/-

364 pp • Rs. 175/-

144 pp • Rs. 60/-

150 pp • Rs. 80/-

144 pp • Rs. 80/-

296 pp • Rs. 150/-

120 pp • Rs. 68/-
Also available in Hindi

104 pp each
Rs. 36/- each

152 pp • Rs. 125/-   152 pp • Rs. 125/-

124 pp • Rs. 120/-
Coloured Ed. + FREE Tutorial CD

New

Also available in Hindi

New

64 pp • Rs. 72/-

New

64 pp • Rs. 72/-

New

64 pp • Rs. 72/-

New

64 pp • Rs. 72/-

124 pp • Rs. 80/-
Also available in Hindi

5

152 pp • Rs. 96/-

224 pp • Rs. 120/-

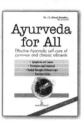

224 pp • Rs. 150/-

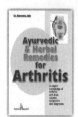

192 pp • Rs. 96/-

112 pp • Rs. 60/-

115 pp • Rs. 80/-

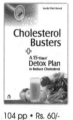

104 pp • Rs. 60/-

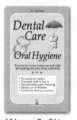

136 pp • Rs. 96/-

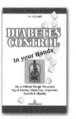

120 pp • Rs. 88/-

104 pp • Rs. 69/-

232 pp • Rs. 90/-

144 pp • Rs. 80/-

128 pp • Rs. 80/-

243 pp • Rs. 160/-

168 pp • Rs. 88/-

136 pp • Rs. 80/-

304 pp • Rs. 120/-

HEALTH REJUVENATING EXERCISES

52 pp • Rs. 24/-

144 pp • Rs. 96/-

152 pp • Rs. 88/-

128 pp • Rs. 96/-

136 pp • Rs. 68/-

428 pp • Rs. 175/-

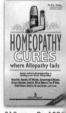

312 pp • Rs. 150/-

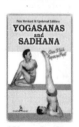

176 pp • Rs. 60/-

180 pp • Rs. 80/-

150 pp • Rs. 68/-

128 pp • Rs. 68/-

242 pp • Rs. 120/-

140 pp • Rs. 96/- (Vo
224 pp • Rs. 135/- (V

20 pp • Rs. 88/-

112 pp • Rs. 60/-
Also in Hindi & Bangla

128 pp • Rs. 48/-
Also in Hindi & Bangla

96 pp • Rs. 48/-

120 pp • Rs. 80/-

176 pp • Rs. 96/-

92 pp • Rs. 120/-

224 pp • Rs. 88/-

232 pp • Rs. 80/-
Also available in Hindi

224 pp • Rs. 80/-

168 pp • Rs. 80/-

96 pp • Rs. 80/-

132 pp • Rs. 96/-

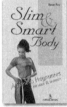
128 pp • Rs. 80/-

192 pp • Rs. 68/-

152 pp • Rs. 80/-

228 pp • Rs. 120/-

76 pp • Rs. 110/-

128 pp • Rs. 80/-

184 pp • Rs. 120/-

124 pp • Rs. 96/-

& many more...

pp • Rs. 60/-

112 pp • Rs. 48/-

144 pp • Rs. 60/-

168 pp • Rs. 72/-

128 pp • Rs. 48/-

120 pp • Rs. 72/-

176 pp • Rs. 88/-

176 pp • Rs. 68/-

Alternative Therapies

136 pp • Rs. 60/-

64 pp • Rs. 48/-

144 pp • Rs. 88/-

240 pp • Rs. 96/-

84 pp • Rs. 60/-

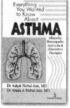
168 pp • Rs. 80/-

224 pp • Rs. 96/-

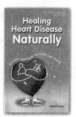
200 pp • Rs. 96/-

180 pp • Rs. 68/-

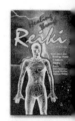
104 pp • Rs. 60/-

120 pp • Rs. 60/-

128 pp • Rs. 68/-

200 pp • Rs. 80/-

128 pp • Rs. 80/-

242 pp • Rs. 120/-

280 pp • Rs. 96/-

304 pp • Rs. 120/-

264 pp • Rs. 150/-

112 pp • Rs. 80/-

112 pp • Rs. 80/-

264 pp • Rs. 108/-

144 pp • Rs. 80/-

168 pp • Rs. 96/-

112 pp • Rs. 68/-

& many more...

Astrology, Palmistry, Hypnotism & Numerology

152 pp • Rs. 96/-

184 pp • Rs. 80/-

200 pp • Rs. 96/-

208 pp • Rs. 125/-

348 pp • Rs. 240/-
Hardbound

142 pp • Rs. 80/-

282 pp • Rs. 88/-

365 pp • Rs. 80/-
Also available in Hindi

264 pp • Rs. 110/-

248 pp • Rs. 150/-

152 pp • Rs. 96/-

160 pp • Rs. 75/-

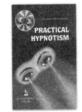

236 pp • Rs. 75/-
Also available in Hindi

107 pp • Rs. 80/-

264 pp • Rs. 150/-

184 pp • Rs. 96/-

222 pp • Rs. 80/-

120 pp • Rs. 80/-

272 pp • Rs. 96/-

160 pp • Rs. 60/-
Also available in Hindi

144 pp • Rs. 60/-

136 pp • Rs. 88/-

144 pp • Rs. 88/-

92 pp • Rs. 72/-

& many more...

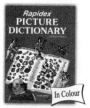

192 pp • Rs. 80/-

136 pp • Rs. 99/-

New

208 pp • Rs. 175/-

264 pp • Rs. 80/-

448 pp • Rs. 175/-

520 pp • Rs. 195/-

Rs. 60/- each

Rapidex Straight to the Point Series

Price: 60/- each

Rapidex Condensed Users Guides

Price: 140/- each

Other Computer Books

The Wap Book	99/-
The Java Book	195/-
Dreamweaver 3	195/-
Low-cost Web Site	225/-
Internet Marketing & Promotions	225/-
Microsoft FrontPage 8	90/-
Microsoft Outlook 2000	125/-
E-Strategy	120/-

240 pp • Rs. 88/-

256 pp Rs. 96/-

208 pp Rs. 96/-

144 pp • Rs. 80/-

128 pp • Rs. 80/-

64 pp • Rs. 30/-

160 pp • Rs. 80/-

144 pp • Rs. 68/-

96 pp • Rs. 68/-

116 pp • Rs. 60/-

120 pp • Rs. 60/-

208 pp • Rs. 160/-

128 pp • Rs. 96/-

128 pp • Rs. 80/-

Religious Books

216 pp • Rs. 150/-

180 pp + 16 Colour
Rs. 96/-

120 pp + 16 Colour
Rs. 96/-

328 pp • Rs. 199/- (H.B.)
Also available in Hindi

Rs. 499/-
pp: 186 • H.B. • Full Colour

180 pp • Rs. 60/-

88 pp • Rs. 80/-

96 pp • Rs. 60/-

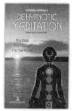

132 pp • Rs. 96/-

Rs. 399/-
pp: 96 • H.B. • Full Colour

224 pp • Rs. 80/-

328 pp • Rs. 96/-

120 pp • Rs. 80/-

136 pp • Rs. 80/-

158 pp • Rs. 80/-

144 pp • Rs. 80/-

112 pp • Rs. 50/-

156 pp • Rs. 80/-

Rs. 499/-
pp: 176 • H.B. • Full Colour

144 pp • Rs. 80/-

104 pp • Rs. 48/-

200 pp • Rs. 60/-

96 pp • Rs. 40/-

Rs. 399/-
pp: 148 • H.B. • Full Colour

Published by HINDOOLOGY BOOKS — An imprint of Pustak Mahal

102 pp • Rs. 60/-

136 pp • Rs. 80/-

152 pp • Rs. 125/-

104 pp • Rs. 60/-

96 pp • Rs. 96/-

144 pp • Rs. 125/-

144 pp • Rs. 80/-
Also in Hindi

120 pp • Rs. 80/-

112 pp • Rs. 60/-

144 pp • Rs. 80/-

168+16 colour pp
Rs. 80/-

160 pp • Rs. 125/-

176 pp • Rs. 96/-

140 pp • Rs. 80/-

86 pp • Rs. 80/-

32 pp each • Rs. 40/- each

192 pp • Rs. 150/-

144 pp • Rs. 80/-

248 pp • Rs. 96/-

296 pp • Rs. 150/-

176 pp • Rs. 80/-

152 pp • Rs. 110/-

112 pp • Rs. 80/-

128 pp • Rs. 80/-
Also available in Hindi

128 pp • Rs. 80/-

144 pp • Rs. 75/-
Also available in Hindi

160 pp • Rs. 120/-

180 pp • Rs. 120/-

13

New

Under the rain tree

176 pp • Rs. 95/-

Bedtime Mailbox

148 pp • Rs. 80/-

The funny side of GOLE

96 pp • Rs. 120/-

NUGGETS of WISDOM

112 pp • Rs. 80/-

New

VINCULUM

260 pp • Rs. 95/-

QUICK BITES for spare moments

224 pp • Rs. 120/-

Curses & Jinxes

164 pp • Rs. 80/-

UNWRITTEN-FLAWS OF INDIAN BUREAUCRACY

248 pp • Rs. 295/-
(Hardbound)

Amusing Anecdotes on Indian Red Tape

176 pp • Rs. 80/-

Over a Cup of Coffee

Musings by V.N. Kakar

244 pp • Rs. 120/-

Over 700 Witty & Humorous Definitions

120 pp • Rs. 80/-

Amusing Encounters of Daily Life

124 pp • Rs. 68/-

MYSTERIOUS MONSTERS OF THE WORLD

112 pp • Rs. 80/-

136 INCREDIBLE COINCIDENCES

128 pp • Rs. 80/-

Endangered Animals of the World

160 pp • Rs. 96/-

DREAMS & PREMONITIONS

152 pp • Rs. 80/-

TRUE Ghosts & Spooky Incidents

136 pp • Rs. 80/-

Mysteries around UFOs & Aliens

174 pp • Rs. 80/-

101 BRAIN TEASERS

152 pp • Rs. 68/-
also in Hindi

501 ASTONISHING FACTS

115 pp • Rs. 60/-
also in Hindi

501 FASCINATING FACTS

104 pp • Rs. 60/-
also in Hindi,
Bangla, Kannada &
Assamese

FUN WITH NUMBERS

115 pp • Rs. 60/-
also in Hindi

112 pp • Rs. 60/-
also in Hindi

MAGIC FOR FUN

112 pp • Rs. 60/-
also in Hindi,
Kannada and Marathi

101 Magic Tricks

112 pp • Rs. 96/-

MAGIC for YOU

124 pp • Rs. 48/-
also in Hindi

MAGIC for CHILDREN

124 pp • Rs. 60/-
also in Hindi

Origin of 101 Everyday Things

180 pp • Rs. 68/-

Strange But True Facts

184 pp • Rs. 80/-

How to solve Crossword Puzzles

104 pp • Rs. 60/-

Sudoku

64 pp • Rs. 50/- each

Children Stories / Pre-School Primers

3 Vols. • pp: 24 each
Rs. 36/- each
Also available in Hindi

2 Vols. • pp: 56 & 60 each
Rs. 60/- each
Also available in Hindi

2 Vols. • pp: 56 each
Rs. 60/- each
Also available in Hindi

pp: 120
Rs. 60/-

pp: 96
Rs. 60/-

pp: 144
Rs. 80/-

96 pp • Rs. 48/-
Also in Hindi

24 pp • Rs. 36/- each
Also available in Hindi

60 pp • Rs. 60/- each
Also available in Hindi

48 pp • Rs. 50/- each
Also available in Hindi

5 Vols. • pp: 60 to 68 each
Rs. 60/- each
Also available in Hindi

Combined Edition
pp: 304 • Rs. 350/-
Also available in Hindi

160 pp • Rs.80/-

120 pp
Rs. 60/-

144 pp • Rs. 60/-
Also available in Hindi

160 pp • Rs. 72/-

115 pp • Rs. 60/-

98 pp • Rs. 72/-

120 pp • Rs. 80/-

32 pp • Rs. 36/- each
Also available in Hindi

128 pp • Rs. 80/-

104 pp • Rs. 68/-

176 pp • Rs. 68/-

144 pp • Rs. 80/-

164 pp • Rs. 80/-

24 pp • Rs. 36/-

Rs. 15/- each
Fully coloured
& illustrated.
Can be wiped off.

15